erspectives in Metropolitan Research VI

ublished with the kind support of:

nded by the Deutsche Forschungsgemeinschaft (DFG, German Research Foundation)
nder the project number ZI 1627/6-1

dvisory Board Members

nnette Bögle (Professor of design and analysis of structures, HCU)
grid Breckner (Professor of urban and regional sociology, HCU)
ernot Grabher (Professor of urban and regional economic studies, HCU)
chen Schiewe (Professor of geoinformatics and geovisualization, HCU)
aus Sill (Professor of drafting and building theory, HCU)
esa Ziemer (Professor of cultural theory and practice, HCU)

ne series "Perspectives in Metropolitan Research" is edited by the Vice President
r Research at HafenCity University, Annette Bögle.

afenCity Universität Hamburg
eferat für Forschung
enning-Voscherau-Platz 1
457 Hamburg
rschung@hcu-hamburg.de

Imprint

© 2021 by jovis Verlag GmbH
Texts by kind permission of the authors.
Pictures by kind permission of the photographers/holders of the
picture rights.

All rights reserved.

Cover: Gabriela Bila Advincula

Editors of this volume:
Raphael Schwegmann, Gesa Ziemer, Jörg Rainer Noennig
Proofreading: Tina Steiger, Rhea-Sandhya Meißner,
Mariangela Pallazi Williams, Kerstin Niemann
Design and layout: abseiten (Mehmet Alatur | Katrin Bahrs)
Design chapter markers: Gabriela Bila Advincula
Lithography: Bild1Druck, Berlin
Printed in the European Union

Bibliographic information published by the Deutsche
Nationalbibliothek
The Deutsche Nationalbibliothek lists this publication in the
Deutsche Nationalbibliografie; detailed bibliographic data are
available on the Internet at http://dnb.d-nb.de

jovis Verlag GmbH
Lützowstraße 33
10785 Berlin

www.jovis.de

jovis books are available worldwide in selected bookstores. Please
contact your nearest bookseller or visit www.jovis.de for information concerning your local distribution.

ISBN 978-3-86859-600-7

Perspectives in Metropolitan Research

Digital City Science

Raphael Schwegmann, Gesa Ziemer
and Jörg Rainer Noennig (eds.)

Contents

II. Working the City

Digital Science

Paradigm Shift: Understanding the Digital Transformation of Cities

Raphael Schwegmann/Jörg Rainer Noennig/
Gesa Ziemer

How will e-Sciences and digital technologies shape future cities — and how are future cities, in turn, shaped by these disciplines? Who are the architects and actors behind these processes? How can citizens and city makers benefit from increasing amounts of data in cities? Driven by a transdisciplinary approach to digital cities, *Perspectives in Metropolitan Research 6* explores the intertwinements of urban development with data science, social science and technology. As a collection of novel research approaches about the digital transformation of cities, this book reflects the notion and role of the city scientist. What assumptions guide contemporary discourses on digital cities? What insights can transdisciplinary research offer for understanding digital urban futures?

The notion of "city science", as historically introduced by different authors like William J. Mitchell (1996), Michael Batty (2013) or Alex Pentland (2015), pinpoints the paradigm shift that information and communication technology (ICT) and data science triggered in urban development. The discipline of Digital City Science thus studies not so much the physical built environment or governance of a city, as traditional urban planning undertakes, but dynamic data-based movements of the city: the flows of people, goods, energies, ideas, and information. It focuses on a city's digital infrastructure, since the internet of things (IoT), the development of urban data platforms, digital urban twin technologies or other collaborative digital tools for decision making and citizen participation effected a fundamental change in contemporary cities and societies.

Addressing this revolution, the City Science group of the MIT Media Lab laid th
scientific and technological groundwork, for establishing City Science as an inter
national research network with the aim of exploring the potential of computer sci
ence, data simulation, and visualisation as drivers of cities. Hence, Digital City Sci
ence aims to offer transformative and novel approaches to academia and applied
research: seeking new points of leverage for urban research and development
while generating innovative theories, practices, and tools for gaining an unprece
dented and in-depth understanding of our cities. The CityScienceLab at HafenCity
University Hamburg has been the first CityScienceLab in this network. It has en
joyed a long-term and successful collaboration with MIT Media Lab since 2015 and
continues to develop the topic of City Science. Our focus is not only on the techno
logical functioning of the city, but also on the added value of data presence for citi
zens and stakeholders. Our contribution is to show how data can be used to meet
the needs of citizens in a digital city. It follows that technologies are never success
ful because they are only technically innovative, but only when people make use of
them and this use enables new forms of collaboration and services.

With this in mind, an international community of researchers from different disci
plines was invited to participate in the annual City Science Summit 2019 in Ham
burg, which was organized from the City Science group of the MIT Media Lab in co
operation with the CityScienceLab at HafenCity University in Hamburg. The summit
takes place once a year at different locations of our international City Science Net
work, and after Andorra (2017) and Shanghai (2018) we were able to hold this con
ference in Hamburg at Elbphilharmonie. In our format we offered a mix, presenting
practical examples of Digital City Science, theoretical approaches, workshops and
the promotion of young talent. The programm curation addressed a diverse audi
ence from science, politics, civil society and industry.

This book summarises some outcomes of the summit and presents various exam
ples of how Digital City Science can be understood by providing a first, non-system
atic introduction to this field. It tentatively outlines key concepts and theories
through visionary essays by international academics that complement and con
trast scientific papers and findings developed during the City Science Summit 2019
The City Science Lab at the HafenCity University Hamburg introduced the concept
of "citizen and stakeholder engagement" as a critical dimension to City Science
Hence, all contributions in this book address and connect key aspects of data tech
nology and citizen science within an urban context. The juxtaposition of these ap
proachesignites a dynamic interplay of possibilities inherent in "digital", "city" and
"science" — stipulating new entanglements and conceptualisations.

Digital

The term digital, above all, indicates that Digital City Science is data-driven. The sheer amount of data generated in urban systems is an immense resource for generating knowledge and gaining insights. City data provide an unprecedented perspective of urban processes; city data provide the key for a deep understanding of cities and how they function. The Latin notion "datum", translated as "given", refers to the wealth of urban data in Digital City Science, and is understood as a given river of urban life and activity. On that basis new solutions for analysing, understanding, and anticipating urban development are revealed. Digital City Science uses data to derive societal and economic values by the creation of decision-support instruments for planning and policy-making (Data to Decisions), skillful information design and data interaction (Data to Visualisation), as well as algorithmic analyses and machine learning (Data to Knowledge).

Cities

In the global urban age cities have turned into massive challenges. Urban growth resulting from demographic and environmental changes, migration and informal settlements and critical states of physical and societal health, means that urban systems of extreme complexity proliferate. Digital City Science responds to these conditions with a holistic approach. From this view cities are considered dynamic systems of multi-layer interactions; living organisms resiliently self-organising, while rarely conforming to visions of master plans. In order to grasp such complex dynamics, Digital City Science provides a powerful tool — and method box — equipped with interactive instruments for analysis, visualisation, and simulation.

Science

Digital City Science engages inter- and transdisciplinary methodologies by combinations of qualitative and quantitative approaches acknowledging that urban challenges cannot be resolved from a mono-disciplinary perspective. Whereas social and cultural perspectives, on the one hand uncover implicit power relations, possibilities for a breadth of citizen engagement and multi-stakeholder participation are opened. On the other hand, rigorous quantitative data reinforce scientific evidence and validity. Statistical models complement discursive approaches with an analysis of urban data science which is non-speculative, human-centric, and community-oriented.

Book Concept: A Juxtaposition of Perspectives

This book addresses current discourses on concepts of the digital by enhancing them with findings from joint research activities of the international City Science network, an initiative by the City Science group of the MIT Media Lab. Its multiperspectivity, however, is both a reflection of the image and values of City Science as well as an invitation to radical innovation. The book intends to initiate a discourse, an exchange of different methods, measures, and materials; a forum of theories, toys, and tools; a debate on power, prestige, and the perfection of—or in—Digital City Science. Contributions discuss digital cities in a diversity of contexts: spanning from environmental change to informality, from community-building to future mobilities—all the while moving the Global South into ever stronger focus. The authors further explore, among others, urban facets of video-gaming, e-planning, or cultural data science.

This volume comprises three parts, each presenting a distinct approach to the interplay of Digital, Cities, and Science by creating a panoramic forum illustrating the abundance of inter- and transdisciplinary perspectives.

I. Science and the City

The first part presents rigorous academic approaches in the format of academic papers discussing case studies, theories, methods, and models that aim to answer the question: "How do we research the Digital City?". With respect to the physical and socio-spatial context of each case study, the contributions in this section acknowledge the geographical range of Digital City Science as a truly global scholarship.

Lisa Reudenbach, Marie Malchow, Luis Alberto Alonso Pastor, and Markus Elkatsh open the first part of the book with an overview of technology and innovation in informal settlements, showing the potential of Digital City Science as a helpful approach for fostering participation in non-western communities of the Global South. Jesús López Baeza, Jörg Rainer Noennig, Vanessa Weber, Arnaud Grignard, Ariel Noyman, Kent Larson, Tri Nguyen-Huu, Sebastian Saxe, and Ulrich Baldauf introduce an agent-based model (ABM) for optimising cruise passenger flows in Hamburg, paving the way for the creation of a digital city twin. GPTS Hemakumara presents a surprising new approach for grassroots participatory mapping, forming the basis for geo-spatial e-Planning in Sri Lanka. Vanessa Weber contributes an interview with the data curation expert Vishal Kumar on the specific processes of curating cultural data for cities. Addressing the field of urban data visualisation, Ariel Noyman and Kent Larson present "A Deep Image of the City", a result of algorithmic and machine-learning processing of urban data. Increasingly relevant in the Covid-19 context, the paper by Evgenia Yosifova and Jörg Pohlan discusses the dialectics of public health and data in the urban realm. Shedding light on the relationship between open data and participation, Rosa Thoneick, Till Degkwitz, and Claudius Lieven present the Urban Data Hub of Hamburg and its importance for "Citizen Science". Their work investigates theoretical implications of citizen participation in terms of theories of democracy, public law, and political science, as well as making claims for legitimisation and representative inclusion in the digital city.

Future and the City

ontributions in the second part of the book transcend the scope of rigorous academ-
research by presenting programmatic visions. These scenarios—whether utopian
dystopian—creatively challenge the academic papers of the preceding section by
eir polemic and essayistic formats: what kind of future Digital City can we imagine?
their article "Of Zeros and Ones", Nikita John, Lisa Harseim, Gionatan Vignola, and
athrin Zengerling explore choices that shape the zero-carbon and digital city of
morrow. Alina Nazmeeva illustrates the perspective of "The City as a Videogame".
 environmental dimension is added by Sebastian Meyer, Inga Schlegel and Jochen
hiewe who envision a far-reaching usage of weather data for smart cities, show-
g how data stories, urban visual narratives, and storytelling can support such
olution. Hilke Marit Berger, Patrick Postert, Imanuel Schipper, and Anna E. M. Wolf
esent a project called PAKOMM describing the creation of a future scenario in
hich VR and AR technologies play a significant role.

Working the City: City Science Summit 2019

he third section of this volume summarises the results of the workshops during
e City Science Summit in Hamburg. As an international forum on cutting-edge
search and technologies, the summit was entitled "Cities WITHOUT" and offered
teractive workshops exploring the contributions of digital technologies to cities
ithout conventional infrastructures or technologies, such as transportation, water
d sewage systems, or planning rules. For these scenarios, new urban decision-
aking designs, tools, and theories, in pursuit of improving the liveability and inno-
tion of places, was sought. Thus, the third section presents outcomes from work-
op sessions and panels at the 2019 summit, addressing the central question: how
n we improve cities without […]?

sults from the following workshops were selected: "Mobility WITHOUT Noise"
Wolfgang Gruel, André Landwehr); "Art WITHOUT Humans" (Sarah Adam, Hilke Berg-
, Vanessa Weber); "Cities WITHOUT Privacy" (Christian Kurtz, Florian Wittner, Mattis
cobs); a session series on informality: 1. "Development WITHOUT Formality"/2. "In/
rmality WITHOUT Bias"/3. "Hamburg WITHOUT Borders" (Lisa Reudenbach, Marie
alchow, Luis Alberto Alonso Pastor, Markus Elkatsha); "Data Chains WITHOUT
hained Data" (Daniel Mondino, Emiliya Popova, David Ehrenreich, Suleiman Alhadidi
d Christian Jara Figueroa); "Arrival WITHOUT Departure" (Jan Barski, Benedikt
eitzer) and "Smart WITHOUT Culture" (Jens Bley, Martin Niggemann).

eferences

tty, M. (2013). *The New Science of Cities*. Cambridge, MA.
itchell, W.J. (1996). *City of Bits: Space, Place, and the Infobahn*. Cambridge, MA.
ntland, A. (2015). *Social Physics: How Social Networks Can Make Us Smarter*. London.

Silence and the City

. Technology & nnovation in Informal Settlements

isa Reudenbach/Marie Malchow/
uis Alberto Alonso Pastor/Markus Elkatsha

ties have existed for centuries, functioning as centres of human cultural, social, d economic development and interaction. With the ongoing process of rapid ur-nisation, this global urban landscape is undergoing radical changes. In 2018, the solute number of people living in slums or informal settlements grew to over one llion, now representing 23.5% of the global urban population (UN Statistics Divi-n 2019). By 2050, 68% of the world's population is projected to live in cities. Natu-l population growth and high rates of rural-to-urban migration will cause urban eas to experience a growth of 2.5 billion people, with nearly 90% of this increase king place in Asia and Africa (UN Department of Economic and Social Affairs 19). In these fast-growing regions, between 50–70% of urban dwellers live in ms and informal settlements, making this the predominant form of urbanisa-n (UN-Habitat 2016, p. 157). Watson's review (2009, p. 2263) of relevant literature ncludes that informal urbanisation "is now the norm and no longer the excep-n".

In view of these unprecedented processes, this article explores the interplay of formal urbanisation with digital innovations and new developments in urban anning. It examines the potential for supporting local stakeholders in leveraging portunities of informality and mitigating its risks. In four case studies, grassroots tiatives and their use of digital innovations for purposes of community empower-ent, participation, and visibility are analysed.

ormal Urbanisation

contrast to planned modern cities whose urban form developed with the indus-al revolution, such as New York, London, Paris, Berlin, and Tokyo, currently, global urban growth is occurring without formal planning. There are many terms used to describe settlements shaped by informal urbanisation, such as: self-built communities, slums, squats, favelas, informal settlements, townships, barrios, or the like. First impressions of informal settlements, in many cases evoke images of, for example, overcrowded neighbourhoods with poor living conditions and street vendors selling sunglasses, snacks, or other oddments. We think of conditions that are irregular, uncontrolled, unplanned, illegal, unregulated, undocumented, or unregistered. Informal urbanisation is usually associated with the lack of something—such as services, space, land tenure, and access; or the lack of formal control over planning, design, and construction. Most descriptions are based on physical features, land tenure, quality of settlement, compliance with formal spatial plans, and the context of a settlements' establishment (Suhartini and Jones 2019, p. 231). UN-Habitat uses the following characterisation: "A slum household consists of one or group of individuals living under the same roof in an urban area, lacking one more of the following amenities: access to basic services, durable structural quality of housing, sufficient living area, the security of tenure" (2011, p. 33). Furthermore UN-Habitat (2016, p. 78) describes a lack of access to equal social rights—including basic public services, goods, and amenities—as the defining and most visible characteristic of informal settlements.

Whereas informality was commonly used to define an aspect of the economy, it prevails in describing phenomena in multiple sectors, including: housing, infrastructure, economy, citizenship, or transport. Also, it depicts various economic, social, and spatial processes in urban development (Herrle and Fokdal 2011, p. 3 f.).

Informality is attributed to many causes, "including low-income levels, unrealistic urban planning, a lack of serviced land and social housing, and a dysfunctional legal system" (Fernandes 2011, p. 2). Meijer (2018, p. 40) identifies "incomplete bureaucracies, failing tax collection systems, and corruption" as reasons why local governments lack the resources and planning capacity to provide infrastructures and services. More broadly Obermayr (2017, p. 168 f.) depicts local realities within a global context: besides having to deal with massive urban growth, most city budgets are further strained by the pressure of integration into the global economy, alongside strong interurban competition. Democratisation and decentralisation processes have not only increased power at the local level, but have also added financial obligations and time-consuming processes, leaving cities with fewer resources to tackle the increasing demands posed by "infrastructures, services, comprehensive planning, slum upgrading, or poverty alleviation" (Obermayr 2017, p 168 f.). Also, Roch and van Ballegooijen (2019, p. 24 f.) see "a dangerous combination of unpreparedness, denial, ignorance, and a strong ideological component, related to how political elites see the role of the state as a provider of public goods".

ost of these conceptualisations assume that the existence of informality is, in
ome way, caused by an absent state. Kreibich (2016), however, introduces a distinc-
on between different types of informality that exist within the scope of the state.
hile a strong public authority affects informality by fostering exclusion, a weak
ublic authority affects informality through its fragility. A third type of informality
xists in certain parts of cities that remain uncontrolled by the public hand.
N-Habitat (2016) further highlights that in many cases it is public authorities
emselves who contribute to informality, using it to their own benefit and advan-
ge. Rocco and van Ballegooijen (2019, p. 24 f.) conclude: "...the state selectively in-
udes or excludes groups of people depending on the power they yield in the polit-
al process and the local societal model". Whereas Alfaro d'Alençon et al. (2018, p.
) looked at informality from the perspective of state-society relations, noting that
he idea of the state and of its role is in flux (especially that of the nation-state),
ving rise to a wide array of governance regimes".

hile informality is mostly associated with underdevelopment and poverty, many
udies show how informal processes are also "a major way that housing is provid-
 for much of the world's population", and that "the informal economy is an im-
rtant source of employment, income, and business in many cities" (UN-Habitat
16, p. 132). The research on Cairo by Tarbush (2012, p. 172) finds that "far from being
 indication of underdevelopment, [informality] has been a rational response by
irenes to population growth and housing shortages." As Dovey (2012, p. 385) accu-
tely summarises: "[P]overty is a problem, and informality is often the means by
hich poverty is managed by the poor". Alfaro d'Alençon et al. (2018, p. 61) analyse
veral studies demonstrating how governments, businesses, and high and mid-
e-income residents use urban informality to the same extent as the urban poor
 marginalised. However, they benefit from informality through their financial, so-
al, or political power—while the marginalised may experience worse conditions,
gher prices, and increased vulnerability through their informality.

e phenomenon of informal urban practices is also on the rise in the global north,
 the wake of recession austerity and growing inequality after the 2008 global fi-
ncial crisis. A deficit of basic services in residential housing in Greece, squatting
 buildings in Spain, or the conversion of shacks and garages in the United King-
m, are only some of the examples documented by Alfaro d'Alençon et al. (2018, p.
 f.).

cco and van Ballegooijen (2019, p. 4) identified two perspectives on urban infor-
ality. The first associates informality with political exclusion, inequality, and pov-
ty, as caused by a democratic deficit and ineffective bureaucracies. The second
rspective sees urban informality as emancipatory—a practice of fostering au-
nomy, entrepreneurship, and bottom-up democracy. Similarly, Alfaro d'Alençon

et al. (2018, p. 61) highlight the capacity of flexibility, adaptation, and resilience, i
contrast to informality, as a survival strategy. The emancipatory perspective, whic
at times may be romanticising or aestheticizing informality, carries the risk of im
peding the necessary policy interventions to ensure equal standards for all settle
ments and citizens.

Such policy approaches cover a broad spectrum, including negligence, eviction
abandonment, regulatory enforcement, social housing construction, integratio
improvement, resettlement, and upgrading (UN-Habitat 2016, p. 132). While som
policies have been successful in improving the living conditions of the urban poc
the overall growth of informal settlements prevails. In addition to the reasons di
cussed above, another set of authors explores the different ways in which peopl
societies, and economies benefit from informality. Davis (2006), for example de
scribes "slumlords" who own or control entire slums—collecting rent or protectio
money while being backed by political elites, while the documentation collected k
UN-Habitat (2016) describes how slums provide a large share of cheap labour fc
the formal sector. Upgrading informal settlements therefore poses the risk of in
creasing the cost of housing, forcing the displacement of people.

Herrle & Fokdal (2011) depict the informality discourse within a triangular logic-
comprised of power, legitimacy, and resources which are constantly re-negotiate
in the production of urban space. Many authors (Suhartini and Jones 2019; Alfa
d'Alençon et al. 2018; Dovey and King 2011; Roy 2009) agree that informality is n
simply the opposite of the formal, but consider it a complex concept with mar
hybrid forms, which cannot—by default—be considered positive or negative. Rat
er than a binary of opposites, informality is understood as a continuum. In th
view, the continuum exists in all cities, as a toleration, negotiation, and contest
tion of formal and informal arrangements, and a mix of formal and informal urba
development processes. In most cases, different typologies of governance overla
intersect, and co-evolve.

Digital Innovation in Urban Planning
In light of unprecedented global urbanisation, and the resulting diversity of info
mal urban forms and processes in daily life, new planning methods and tools a
needed for an urbanisation beneficial to human development.

Traditionally, urban planning is considered a technical and political process in r
gards to land-use, the built environment, and infrastructure, in the interest of pu
lic welfare (American Planning Association 2015). Douay (2018, p. xv) describes th
goal of urban planning as making "plans to regulate land-use and guide growth k
defining zones, building densities, and locations for the installation of commun
facilities". However, in a context of growing informality, Rocco and van Ballegooije

2019, p. 18) depict "the friction between the role of planning as an instrument of oppression [...] and as an enabler of participation and an instrument of redistribution". Here, new technologies offer interesting opportunities to fill existing gaps, address complex urban problems, and support the planning process, all within the enabling role".

The smart city as a conceptual idea and development is based on the use of information and communication technology (ICT) (Shen & Li 2018, p. 1) in order to "improve the quality of life for urban citizens by improving the quality and performance of urban services, such as transport, utilities, energy, and so on—while reducing resource consumption, waste, and costs" (Thornbush and Golubchikov 2020, pp. 6–7). Thornbush and Golubchikov (2020, pp. 1, 52) state that new technologies are being used to "foster efficiency and organisation" as never before; considering them as a "meta-factor" in smart city initiatives. Since the mid-2000s, cities, wishing to become smart, cultivate markets for technology, particularly in the domain of computing (Thornbush and Golubchikov 2020, p. 4). Components of such a smart development include shared mobility, autonomous transportation operations, digital financial transactions, and security systems. Furthermore, this includes migration of activities into cyberspace (e.g. public services) which lead to a "dematerialising of city activities" (Geertman et al. 2019, p. 4; Thornbush and Golubchikov 2020, p. 6).

With the rise in smart city methodologies and the Internet of Things (IoT), over the course of the last decades, the requirements for municipalities have increased immensely, putting pressure on local governments to optimise. "In an era marked by competition between major cities, the city should be smart or digital, as well as sustainable, creative, and resilient" observes Douay (2018, p. xi). While further contributing to this competition, specific indices take on particular importance in ranking cities by their performance. One example is the IESE Cities in Motion Index (CIMI) developed by the Business School of the University of Navarra, comprised of 26 "smartness" indicators, ranking 174 cities in 80 countries along categories of sustainability, social cohesion, connectivity, and innovation (Cities in Motion 2019).

Recently, data collection systems have become more powerful by sensing competencies and automation. With increasing numbers of devices connected to the internet, it is possible to generate "big data" on "almost every facet of urban life" (Thornbush & Golubchikov 2020, p.1). Big data can facilitate urban analysis in many fields, enabling a better understanding of social trends and the environment, offering the possibility to subsequently organise services more efficiently on the basis of better-informed decisions (Geertman et al. 2019, p. 4; Thakuriah et al. 2017, pp. 1–2, 9). Thus, Geertman et al. (2019, p. 4) describe data as "the new oil" of the digital age.

While technological progress opens new possibilities for analysing, understanding, and improving urban processes, it also changes fundamental practices of the planning discipline (Douay 2018, p. xiii). Therefore, there is a need for urban planners, managers, decision-makers, as well as citizens to be adequately equipped with the knowledge, and understanding to deal with big data (Thakuriah et al. 2017, pp. v–vi; Geertman et al. 2019, p. 6; Chakraborty et al. 2015, p. 74).

Furthermore, the use of technology is determined by its affordability: not all city governments are able to invest in advanced technologies in order to address massive urban growth or socio-economic issues on a city-wide level (Thornbush and Golubchikov 2020, p. 49). Thus, technologies pose the risk of augmenting social inequalities, since advantaged groups have disproportionately greater accessibility (Thakuriah et al. 2017, p. 7), rather than instigating collaborative planning approaches. In this context, Dodman (2017, pp. 3–4) describes how the use of technology perpetuates injustice with official data collection often failing to include informalities as it applies to the example of housing or labour. This occurrence, despite the high proportion of informal systems in many fast-growing cities, creates continued discrepancies in statistical representation. In addition, there is a risk that those in control of new technologies and data—be it governments, or in many cases, large corporations—(mis-)use this power to control and/or oppress certain demographics (Douay 2018, p. xvi; Thornbush and Golubchikov 2020, p. 54; Geertman et al. 2019, p. 4). This raises the question of who has access to partaking in the (digital) decision making processes, which are (re)shaping our cities.

In many cases, informal systems function outside of formal urban planning practices. This is where digital planning tools, if used fairly, offer potential for greater public participation in pursuit of a more just decision-making process; for example, with the widespread use of individual mobile phones, possibilities for data collection are unprecedented (Geertman et al. 2019, p.3). It is crucial to gain a better understanding, and make use of, existing data in informal systems in order to include and empower all stakeholders in collaborative planning processes, thereby addressing current challenges (Chakraborty et al. 2015, p. 74).

MIT and HCU Collaborate to Learn About Innovation in Informal Settlements

Researchers in the MIT Media Lab's *City Science group* and HafenCity University *CityScienceLab* learn how novel innovations emerge in informal communities, and how these transformative ideas are improving the quality of life in many parts of the world. This ongoing learning process is based on direct collaboration with informal communities together with a number of institutions (NGOs, universities, governments, etc.), focusing on how informal communities are turning data into meaningful action and impact on the ground.

While informality is often considered in negative terms—characterised as lacking in innovation, cultural contribution, economic viability, technological advancement, or governmental robustness—collaborations with informal communities demonstrate the breadth of knowledge that can be gathered about innovative technological solutions in solving local challenges. Many of these solutions are contributing to people's well-being, often proving more efficient than formal solutions. So how can we stimulate existing community values with new technologies in order to ensure healthier, richer, safer, and more autonomous informal communities? Applying technologies in informal communities, has the potential to be a powerful tool in shaping urban environments around the world. As with most facets of contemporary life, technology is reshaping the future of work and manner in which cities are thought about. Let's take a look at how this applies to informal settlements.

Case Studies—Digital Innovation for Informal Settlements

The following demonstrates four examples, spanning three continents, of how data and technology are used for fostering innovation, basic services, and empowerment in informal settlements by means of data gathering, analysis, and simulation as well as knowledge production and action. The case studies were presented during the *CityScience Summit* in Hamburg, Germany in October 2019, examine challenges based on components of smart development from: (1) material and mobility flow analysis, in formal and informal communities, as factors enhancing liveability in Cairo, Egypt; to (2) assessing safety and security by means of art and music education on the outskirts of Guadalajara, Mexico; and (3) empowering residents of informal settlements in Port Harcourt, Nigeria to voice and imagine, plan and build their neighbourhoods in new and sustainable ways through media advocacy, urban planning, and litigation; to (4) innovative, local community entrepreneurs joining forces with formal start-ups for the provision of urban solutions in healthcare, waste management, and access to potable water in Delhi, India. All of the case studies illustrate situations at the intersection of the formal and the informal.

Cairo: Enhancing Liveability through Resource Efficiency

The continuous growth of cities and the emergence of new ones, is an extremely resource-intensive process that can affect and accelerate climate change and contribute to the depletion of resources. In order to address this, and also improve the quality of urban life, many experts call for the decoupling of resource intensity, economic and urban development—especially for cities in the Global South. Fostering resource efficiency in cities is also an essential aspect of achieving many of the UN Sustainable Development Goals (SDGs) as well as guidelines set by the New Urban Agenda (NUA). The case study in Egypt, demonstrates how a strong "analysis" component in the data-to-action cycle can contribute to better material management and resource efficiency.

To this end, Cairo University has undertaken exhaustive fieldwork and communit engagement in two districts in Cairo. Data were collected in the informal district o Imbaba, one of the most densely populated areas of Greater Cairo, and the formall designed, and built district of Zamalek, a garden city on the Nile. The goal was t measure material quantities in order to assess resource flows within the differen districts, as well as compare and correlate data between the two different areas i the city. In-depth surveys were conducted to quantify the urban metabolisms of th communities by comprehensive lists of material streams collected in each localit This provided an understanding of material flow—from use, to reuse, recycling an finally to landfills, i.e. from source to sink. This view of consumption considers urba systems as an ecosystem where material flows are interconnected. At present, th data collected on this topic in Egypt are minimal, therefore Cairo University devel oped a system of identifying and categorising resource flows at a dwelling leve These data are analysed in the Urban Metabolism Information System (UMIS), framework developed by the NGO *Ecocity Builders* and its associated partners a British Columbia Institute of Technology (BCIT) through a joint project with Cair University (Attia and Khalil 2015, p. 669).

This is an example of data gathering by means of a community engagement pro cess: the collection was conducted through a combination of crowd-sourced dat and household audits, coupled with the knowledge of experts in analysing an aggregating sample audits. The research relied on a bottom-up approach for th aggregation of local resource-flow data, offering an alternative to the government data collected on a national level which is oftentimes inaccurate especially in infor mal communities. To visualise this information, the collected data were generate into Sankey diagrams, offering a visual evaluation of the complex systems making up the urban metabolism for material flows.

Through this analysis, the researchers were able to develop evidence-based argu ments to counter the misconception that informal areas are burdensome, in con trast to planned districts being considered efficient. In addition, the research show cased the interweave between formal and informal systems, by e.g. informal wast pickers contributing a recycling rate of 70–80 % of the total collected waste withi the investigated formal district (Khalil and Al-Ahwal 2020, p. 12). Furthermore, th study proposes a number of systemic strategies that outline resource efficiency o the individual, the building, the district, and the city level, offering considerable in sight into the scale of consumption in various urban areas.

The urban metabolism study is another example of the data-to-action process an of possibilities for empowering informal communities. A bottom-up, multi-layere data collection process combined with an in-depth analysis of material flows wa visualised in Sankey diagrams which allowed for the acquisition and spread o knowledge about resource efficiency strategies; and served to debunk biases against informal communities.

Guadalajara: Creating Opportunities for Crime Prevention through Community Engagement and Data Generation

In *Lomas Del Centinela*, Guadalajara, Mexico, data gathering and data generation offered insight into the challenges, strategies, and actors involved in the promotion of crime and violence in the community, and generated indicators for measuring the potential impact of interventions. In the second step, potential interventions were simulated based on the collected data and then applied in consensual processes with the community.

Lomas del Centinela is an informal settlement of 5,400 inhabitants located in a region defined as being of "priority attention" by the municipality of Zapopan. The community is located between two contrasting neighbourhoods. On one side is Las Mesas, where people live in conditions of poverty, suffering from hunger and malnutrition, and are exposed to crime and violence. On its other side is Bosques de San Isidro, a wealthy neighbourhood, known as *Las Cañadas*. The recently settled, informal community has a very young population, with the age of the oldest inhabitants ranging between 20–30 years, and a high proportion of children on the verge of adolescence. This offers an opportunity for implementing actions that allow a new orientation through education and art for the prevention of youth involvement in illegal activities.

The University of Guadalajara in collaboration with MIT *CityScience Group*, the local NGO *Circle of Friends*, and a diverse group of community stakeholders, hosted a series of workshops in the neighbourhood of *Lomas del Centinela* to identify major challenges in the area. Workshops and site visits were organised to collect preliminary data, while simulation models probed and evaluated potential interventions within the community.

Parallel to the workshops, quantitative and qualitative data were collected in collaboration with the National Research Center *Cinvestav* at Guadalajara Campus. Cooperating with local stakeholders made it possible to define indicators of safety, security, and identify the places and typologies of violence. With this data, an agent-based model (ABM) was developed, using the modelling and simulation development environment GAMA. In order to feed the simulation with a realistic set of data, a database was generated based on collective knowledge derived from the local community and related to incidences of crime and violence. This is a joint collaborative effort by community members, local NGOs, and academic bodies researching in the community and working to understand informal growth.

With the overall goal of mitigating everyday violence in the community, workshop identified the following actions and recommendations: empower committed local leaders, strengthen community organisations and empower women, create incentives for addressing violence and safety, and strengthen opportunities for disadvantaged people.

The knowledge gained from the data collection and simulation was put into action by various local stakeholders such as NGOs, universities, and the municipality. From this, a number of interventions in response to violence and crime in the community were developed, including: an art workshop; an urban agriculture project; and a community dining room, where children and their parents have the opportunity to engage in training and develop work skills, distant from the everyday violence.

The University of Guadalajara initiated an urban literacy programme with a group of children between the ages of 3–14 years, with the goal of promoting the acquisition of values, attitudes, and behaviours that contribute to establishing a culture of respect in the community. The programme is based on playful activities and literacy practices that foster the construction of the children's identity as subjects of change, within their social environment.

This case study demonstrates the process from data collection to simulation knowledge, and action. Stakeholders from the community and the University of Guadalajara collaborated to collect quantitative and qualitative data, used to identify indicators for safety and security, such as statistics on crime and community challenges. The collected data were used for generating simulations in order to better understand the processes, behaviours, and reasons behind security and safety issues. This knowledge was then directly introduced to the local community with the aim of empowering its inhabitants to create change, e.g., through preventative measures for adolescents.

Port Harcourt: The Human City Project—A Community-driven Media, Architecture, Urban Planning, and Human Rights Movement

It is estimated that by the year 2050, an additional 210 million people will live in Nigeria's cities. Currently, 70% of urban dwellers in Nigeria live in slums. With growing inequality and exclusion, countless Nigerian city dwellers lack access to basic services, leaving many vulnerable to abuses of human rights and deprived of access to public services, essential for realising their economic, social, and cultural rights. By 2050, 70% of Nigeria's urban dwellers will be under the age of 19. The struggle for equal rights is therefore most pressing in Nigeria's slums and must be led by young people. Across most of today's world, being a young, disadvantaged slum-dweller is the "core urban condition"(CMAP 2020b).

As the interactive community mapping platform, CMAP (2020a) describes:

In 2009, the homes and businesses of 19,000 people in Port Harcourt were reduced to rubble over the course of one weekend. As the displaced residents picked through the debris of their former lives, the governor declared his vision to transform Port Harcourt into a "garden city." Two years later the site remains derelict and overgrown. About 480,000 people live in waterfronts that fringe the city. All of them are threatened with forced eviction. They also suffer from the violence of prejudicial policing. At present, waterfront communities are not featured on municipal maps, nor in the plans drawn up for the city's development. They are underrepresented and misrepresented in the mainstream media. Residents feel that lack of a public voice and prejudicial narratives about their neighbourhoods contribute to the impunity with which state security forces routinely violate their fundamental rights.

Furthermore, the project (CMAP 2020a) portrays its activities in Port Harcourt as:

The Human City Project in Port Harcourt combines media advocacy, urban planning, and litigation to help residents of informal settlements imagine, plan, and build their neighbourhoods in new and sustainable ways. By means of telling their stories on film, on-air, and in the court, charting their realities on maps, and describing their visions in urban action plans, these communities are changing lives and shaping their city.

The community movement in Port Harcourt is an illustrative example of the data-to-action cycle. Quantitative and qualitative data were collected through community mapping and enumeration, covering aspects like housing, basic services, and infrastructure in addition to socio-economic data. This is complemented by qualitative data from urban-action-planning workshops with community members. Another source of qualitative data comes from the youth who are part of the media team, who used methods of storytelling to collect narratives from community members about daily life, local history, and visions for the future. The data from different community sources were then turned into action. The data was prepared, analysed, and partially visualised on the "narrative geographies" platform, which is openly accessible to community members, urban stakeholders, and the general public. By making this unique combination of hard data (maps, access to infrastructure and services, urban action plans) and soft data (stories, songs, visions, and pictures) publicly available, the community is given a voice, visibility, and empowerment. Complementing the online platform, is a community radio station, along with government advocacy efforts, which make use of the collected data to advocate for community rights and services.

Delhi: Connecting the "Formal" and the "Informal"

In Delhi, the *CityScienceLab@India* analyses how the government, collaboratin
with citizens, industrial and other partners, is embracing knowledge and data gen
erated by informal solutions in order to address medical, waste, and water cha
lenges in formal and informal neighbourhoods. Social movements and start-up
are emerging as a result of formal and informal synergies, acting to address imme
diate challenges in the community with the help of technical innovations. The la
examined technology as a facilitator for nurturing public-private partnership
with the aim of building a governance model that allows for the mutualism be
tween formality and informality, in order to tackle urban challenges and develo
solutions. To do this, it examined three specific projects in the fields of healthcar
waste management, and safe water provision that expertly illustrate the synerg
between diverse actors:

a) Mohalla Clinics

Mohalla clinics are single-doctor community clinics providing primar
care (the Hindi word mohalla translates to neighbourhood) that emerge
from an informal innovation within the local community. The principa
healthcare problems in Delhi include defective primary healthcare se
vices, overcrowded public hospitals, and some of the lowest rates of healt
insurance coverage in the world. The clinics directly address these prob
lems by offering quick services, free of charge. Mohalla clinics operate a
flexible times and engage public and private actors. They are managed b
community volunteers, who also help in spreading health awareness. Doc
tors gather data by means of electronic medical records (EMR) for documen
tation and referral, and oftentimes provide medicine using automate
machines.

b) Kabadiwalla Connect

Kabadiwalla Connect is an interface between informal scrap dealers an
formal processing units from the government. The waste challenges i
Delhi stem, among other causes, from a lack of interaction and collabora
tion between formal and informal waste collection systems. Therefore
they are defined by a high degree of inefficiency. Kabadiwalla Connect use
ICT and IoT to provide a platform for facilitating a more efficient wast
management system by integrating informal stakeholders—i.e., informa
local scrap shops and waste aggregators—into the formal waste collectio
and recycling supply chain. The platform is based on mapping tools tha
provide data on informal as well as formal waste infrastructure. Trackin
tools guarantee traceability of different actors in the supply chain, as well a
offering hyperlocal reverse-logistics solutions in connection with informa
scrap shops to increase the value of the sourced material. The project aim

to lead to a fairer money transfer throughout the supply chain and thus to improved conditions for its informal actors (Kabadiwalla Connect 2020).

c) Sarvajal Water ATM
Delhi's main challenges in regards to water are inaccessible and contaminated drinking water, rampant water-borne diseases, and inefficient water resource management. Sarvajal Water ATM improves the availability, proximity, quality, and quantity of water for so-called beyond-the-pipe communities in Delhi, disconnected from public water systems. It serves as a decentralised, community-level solution providing automated water vending machines that offer 24/7 access to safe drinking water, at a cost of 1 cent per litre. This locally operated social enterprise, uses purification technology at the water source. As a centrally managed service, it is accessible by means of a smart card, ensuring price transparency and quality accountability. Both water quality as well as every pay-per-use transaction are remotely tracked. The project contributed to opportunities of sustainable community livelihoods by partnering with local operators and community-based organisations.

These examples demonstrate the potential of integrating a diverse set of actors at the interface of formal and informal processes. They show how these actors develop new technologies and methods for improved living conditions, while fostering economic activity in informal settlements, and reducing critical urban problems such as energy and resource consumption, congestion, and pollution. In accordance with the data-to-action cycle, all the projects make use of technology in gathering and analysing data, using the knowledge gained to improve their services to communities and thereby fostering their independence and empowerment.

In reference to the previously reviewed literature, the research demonstrates how the distinction between the formal and the informal is not sharp—but rather fuzzy, complex, and multi-layered, and that solutions to urban problems are, in fact, often found within spaces where formality meets informality. It is here—where innovation happens across sectors, scales, and stakeholders—that urban solutions are found at the intersection of people, providers, and policymakers.

Conclusion—Opportunities for Technology and Innovation in Informal Settlements
The literature review at the beginning of this article suggests a bias, that formality is positively associated and informality negatively—when in fact, neither captures the complexity of the phenomenon nor provides adequate application to urban development processes. The case studies in Delhi and Cairo confirm this observation. In Cairo, the research proved that the informal settlement was more resource-efficient than the formal urban development. Also, in Delhi, it was found that gaps in

public services are being filled by collaborations forged between informal and formal actors. Therefore, the question should not be whether a development, or process is formal or informal, but rather what should be considered is whether it is working well, or contributing to the quality of life in a community.

The second part of the article highlights the potential inherent in new technologies for urban planning and city development, as enabled by the unprecedented scale and resolution of geo-information, allowing new insights into informal settlements. New technologies offer new opportunities for participation and empowerment by means of crowd-sourcing data collection and access to new forms of communication and visibility. These new developments, however, also give rise to unprecedented challenges and risks. These include the emergence of new inequalities; marginalisation, through unequal access to new technologies; and risk of the misuse of data and technology for purposes of oppression and control by governments and companies. The four case studies presented here showcase the opportunities that technological innovation may provide, especially for informal settlements. By turning data into action, real impact is achieved in the development of urban areas, even for those who are not represented on official maps.

In Port Harcourt, Nigeria, qualitative and quantitative data are collected by the community and then visualised via an online platform, broadcast by a community radio, and used to advocate for better services—giving the community a voice, visibility, and empowerment.

In Delhi, India, new governance models at the interface of the formal and informal are developed to improve access to basic services for underserved communities. With the help of new technologies, data are collected and analysed in order to improve service delivery, and so foster economic activity and improve living conditions in informal settlements.

In Cairo, Egypt, bottom-up, multi-layered data collection allowed for an in-depth analysis of material flows, which were then visualised to gain and disseminate knowledge about possible resource efficiency strategies, while debunking prevailing biases against informal communities.

In Guadalajara, Mexico, a diverse set of stakeholders collaborated to collect quantitative and qualitative data on aspects of safety and security in the community. The data were used to generate simulations in order to gain a better understanding of their associated processes, behaviours, and motivations. This knowledge was then re-transferred into the community, to empower inhabitants to create change, in this case through preventive measures for adolescents.

e technology dependent, smart city approach poses the risk of increasing in-
quality and marginalisation of informal settlements. This research demonstrates
w technology and community innovation by different stakeholders may, in fact,
ve positive impacts, strengthening the visibility, voice, empowerment, quality of
e, and access to services of communities within informal settlements around the
orld.

e impulse for this research was set in motion at the *CityScienceSummit* in Ham-
rg in October 2019, where all four case studies were presented in a joint session.
inging these inspiring innovators together has sparked a lot of discussion and
eas, for which we would like to thank Mayra Eugenia Gamboa González, Heba
ah Essam El-Din Khalil, Jyotimitra Raghuvansh, as well as Michael Uwemedimo
r contributing their case studies for this article.

ferences

aro d'Alençon, P., H. Smith, E. Álvarez de Andrés, C. Cabrera, J. Fokdal, and M. Lombard
   (2018). "Interrogating informality: Conceptualisations, practices and policies in the
   light of the New Urban Agenda." *Habitat International 75*, pp. 59–66.
erican Planning Association. (2015). *What Is Planning?*, viewed 10 March 2020,
   https://www.planning.org/aboutplanning/.
tia, S. & and H.A.E. Khalil (2015). "Urban metabolism and quality of life in informal
   areas" in CORP- Competence Center of Urban and Regional Planning ed. *REAL CORP
   2015. PLAN TOGETHER–RIGHT NOW–OVERALL. From Vision to Reality for Vibrant Cities
   and Regions. 20th International Conference on Urban Planning*. Gent, pp. 661–674.
ies in Motion. (2019). *IESE Cities in Motion Index 2019*, viewed 09 February 2020,
   https://blog.iese.edu/cities-challenges-and-management/2019/05/10/iese-cities-in-
   motion-index-2019/.

CMAP (2020a). *What we do*, viewed 1 March 2020, https://www.cmapping.net/.

CMAP (2020b). *Violence by design and other stories*, viewed 1 March 2020, https://www.cmapping.net/violence-by-design-and-other-stories/.

Davis, M. (2006). *Planet of Slums*. London.

Dodman, D. (2017). *Opinion: Why informal settlements are already smart*, viewed on 15 January 2020, https://www.devex.com/news/opinion-why-informal-settlements-are-already-smart-89450.

Douay, N. (2018). *Urban Planning in the Digital Age*. London.

Dovey, K. (2012). "Informal urbanism and complex adaptive assemblage." *International Development Planning Review* 34.4: pp. 371–389.

Dovey, K. and R. King (2011). "Forms of Informality: Morphology and Visibility of Informal Settlements" *Built Environment* 37.1: pp. 11–29.

Fernandes, E. (2011). "Regularization of Informal Settlements in Latin America." *Policy Focus Report Series, Lincoln Institute of Land Policy*, viewed 15 March 2020, https://www.lincolninst.edu/sites/default/files/pubfiles/regularization-informal-settlements-latin-america-full_0.pdf.

Geertman, S., A. Allan, Q. Zhan, and C. Pettit (2019). "Computational Urban Planning and Management for Smart Cities: An Introduction." S. Geertman, Q. Zhan, A. Allan, and C. Pettit ed. *Computational Urban Planning and Management for Smart Cities*. Cham.

Herrle, P., J. Fokdal (2011). "Beyond the Urban Informality Discourse: Negotiating Power, Legitimacy and Resources." *Geographische Zeitschrift* 99.1: pp. 3–15.

Kabadiwalla Connect (2020). *Decentralised waste management and waste-collection solutions for cities in the developing world — powered by the informal sector*, viewed 26 February 2020, https://www.kabadiwallaconnect.in/.

Khalil, H.A.E. and A. Al-Ahwal (2020). "Re-understanding Cairo through urban metabolism: Formal versus informal districts resource flow performance in fast urbanizing cities." *Journal of Industrial Ecology*, pp.1–17.

Kreibich, V. (2016). "The mode of informal urbanisation: Reconciling social and statutory regulation in urban land management." M. Waibel and C. McFarlane ed. *Urban Informalities. Reflections on the Formal and Informal*. London.

Meijer, M. (2018). *Community-led, Government-fed and Informal. Exploring planning from below in depopulating regions across Europe.* (Dissertation) Nijmegen.

Obermayr, C. (2017). *Sustainable City Management*. Cham.

Rocco, R. and J. van Ballegooijen (2019). The *Routledge handbook on informal urbanization*. New York.

Roy, A. (2009). "Why India Cannot Plan Its Cities: Informality, Insurgence and the Idiom of Urbanization." *Planning Theory* 8.1: pp. 76–87.

Shen, Z. (2018). "Overview: Big Data Support for Urban Planning and Management in China." Z. Shen and M. Li ed. *Big Data Support of Urban Planning and Management. The Experience in China*. Cham.

Suhartini, N. and P. Jones (2019). *Urban Governance and Informal Settlements*, Cham.

Tarbush, N. (2012). "CAIRO 2050: URBAN DREAM OR MODERNIST DELUSION?" *Journal of International Affairs* 65.2: pp. 171–186.

Thakuriah, P.V., N. Tilahun and M. Zellner (2017). "Introduction to Seeing Cities Through Big Data: Research, Methods and Applications in Urban Informatics." P. Thakuriah, N. Tilahun, and M. Zellner ed. *Seeing Cities Through Big Data. Research Methods and Applications in Urban Informatics*. Cham.

Thornbush, M.J. and O. Golubchikov (2020). *Sustainable Urbanism in Digital Transitions. From Low Carbon to Smart Sustainable Cities*. Cham.

UN Statistics Division (2019). *The Sustainable Development Goals Report 2019*. Goal 11 viewed 24 February 2020, https://unstats.un.org/sdgs/report/2019/goal-11/.

-Habitat (2011). *State of the world's cities 2010–2011: Bridging the urban divide—Overview and key findings,* viewed 24 February 2020, https://sustainabledevelopment.un.org/content/documents/11143016_alt.pdf.

-Habitat (2016). *World Cities Report 2016: Urbanization and development — Emerging futures,* viewed 16 January 2020, https://unhabitat.org/sites/default/files/download-manager-files/WCR-2016-WEB.pdf.

Department of Economic and Social Affairs, Population Division (2019). *World Urbanization Prospects. The 2018 Revision,* viewed 16 January 2020, https://population.un.org/wup/Publications/Files/WUP2018-Report.pdf.

tson, V. (2009). "Seeing from the South: Refocusing Urban Planning on the Globe's Central Urban Issues." *Urban Studies* 46.11: pp. 2259–2275.

, J.J. and Z. Liu (2019). "Micro-and macro-dynamics of open innovation with a quadruple-helix model." *Sustainability* 11: p. 3301.

2. Optimising Cruise Passenger Flow Using ABM: First Steps Towards an Urban Digital Twin[1]

Jesús López Baeza/Jörg Rainer Noennig/
Vanessa Weber/Arnaud Grignard/Ariel Noyman/
Kent Larson/Tri Nguyen-Huu/Sebastian Saxe/
Ulrich Baldauf

1 Cite as: López Baeza, Noennig, Weber, Grignard, Noyman, Larson, Nguyen-Huu, Saxe, Baldauf (2021). Optimising Cruise Passenger Flow Using ABM: First Steps Towards an Urban Digital Twin. In Schwegmann, Ziemer, Noennig (Eds.) Perspectives in Metropolitan Research 6: Digital City Science, Jovis: Berlin, pp. 30–43.

Abstract

This paper reports the application of agent-based models (ABM) for modelling and simulating human flows in the urban environment, using the specific example of the transit of cruise tourists between urban arrival points and cruise terminals in port cities. Findings from the Port City Model project, a collaboration between the Hamburg Port Authority, HCU CityScienceLab and MIT Media Lab's City Science Group, are a first step towards the implementation of a Digital Twin strategy. The project examines flows and routes in the city of Hamburg, where a significant proportion of cruise passengers arrive in the city via the Central Train Station. Due to its size and the sheer number of passengers, Hambu entral Station becomes a major European bottleneck, especially as a point of ultimodal land transportation related to cruise tourism. The spatial orientaon and perception of incoming cruise passengers, making their way to the repective cruise terminals, are identified as a major challenge. Hence, the Port ity Model aims to enhance the comfort and efficiency of cruise tourists in trant by testing alternative mobility scenarios. This research acknowledges that e potential of optimising ports and port-related mobility processes is a main riority and seeks to effect improvement, in relation to the entire city-harbour stem.

ocess Models for Cruise Businesses

ver the past few years, cruise tourism has grown to become one of the fastest xpanding business sectors. Several major port cities such as Hamburg, Marille, Helsinki, or Genoa, in the European context, are reaping benefits from this evelopment, while their urban fabric resiliently tries to respond to the new contions. An imperative quality measure in cruise tourism is the degree of custom- satisfaction. This is largely influenced by the condition, or rather, the quality of ansit as provided by the different modes of transportation, connecting custom- s with their cruise ship. In this context, the processes of embarking and disem- arking in the respective port cities are decisive factors in quality assessments of e cruise experience (Vaggelas and Lagoudis 2010; Bowen and Clarke 2002). The irst impression" upon embarking onto a cruise ship and the "last impression" hen disembarking, play a major role in determining the personal evaluation of e overall cruise experience. Furthermore, these are the critical times at which uise tourism can have a socio-economic impact on the local port city.

his research takes the passenger perspective in examining the processes of uise ship embarkation and disembarkation in port cities. By generating supy-chain modelling of multimodal transfers, in relation to the urban mobility of uise ship passengers, this is analysed. To do so, spatial GIS platform models are eveloped to represent infrastructure, settings, location, and function. Then, ata from external sources are extracted and processed as socio-spatial inforation, and actively applied to the specific localities under scrutiny. In combing the spatial model with the input data, the behaviour of the "agents" involved the process is simulated—deriving the agent-based models (ABMs)—in so, rtraying socio-spatial system behaviours and interactions. By modifying any these inputs, such as, spatial setting or behavioural data of agents, the effect spatial or process planning interventions on the behaviour of the overall sysm can be tested.

is project addresses a major gap in research on cruise economy and planning aggelas and Lagoudis 2010), focusing on synergies of different urban mobility and transportation systems, in addition to generating alternative planning scena ios and predictions—all from the perspective of Digital City Science. The applic tion of ABMs to urban systems, will facilitate an understanding of multi-layere chain processes, as well as predict complex dynamic system scenarios, thus, su porting adequate decision-making by urban planners and managers.

This research utilises interactive hardware platforms and touch-table computers provide visualisations and real-time interactions in order to enhance decision-ma er engagement collaboratively. Similar hardware applications using "tangible us interfaces" (Noyman et al. 2017; Grignard et al. 2018; Noyman 2015; Alonso et 2018) have already been coupled with ABMs to enable easier user-interaction (Alo so et al. 2018; Grignard et al. 2018). An exploratory endeavour by its very nature, involved partners envision this research as kind of first prototype of a more con prehensive, digital city model—an Urban Digital Twin—extrapolating urban pr cess modelling from the scale of a harbour site to the greater urban environmen On a global scale, it could become a blueprint for other cities to model social, ec nomic, or logistics processes.

Hamburg's Bottleneck

The city of Hamburg is undergoing a transformation of its industrial and econom profile, originally based on trading, logistics, and media industries. This transitio especially affects processes associated with business in the Port of Hamburg. Cor plementing the profitability of global container shipping, cruise tourism has b come a major economic driver in recent years, affecting not only the port area, b the entire city (Merk and Hesse 2012). Cruise tourism, which transfers more tha half a million passengers per year (HPA Hafen Hamburg 2019), strongly impac Hamburg's socio-economic fabric, as well as flows of multimodal land transport tion (Merk and Hesse 2012). As the second busiest port in Europe (APAA 2019), t Port of Hamburg features three separate cruise terminals in different location Therefore, this research contends, that Hamburg is suffering from a striking m match, between the capacity of the port, in terms of cruise passengers, and t public transportation infrastructures connecting the urban transfer points wi the three cruise terminals.

Preliminary research conducted with local stakeholders active in the cruise al harbour business indicated that Hamburg's Central Train Station is the greate obstacle to the efficient transfer of cruise tourists. As the busiest train station Germany, and the second busiest in Europe—it serves over 800 long-distan trains, 1,200 commuter trains, and over half a million visitors per day (Schirm 2018). This transportation load, coupled with its position as a nexus between two the city's major districts, and an unfortunate building composition, leads to seve congestion during peak times. In the case of Hamburg Central Station, the size the building structure and the crowds of people are in stark disproportion to o

nother. The building facilities are rather small in relation to the vast flows of people, hence being described as a "bottleneck", "overloaded" or "operating on the edge
of its capacity" (Schirmar 2018; Wen et al. 2017).

Urban planners and traffic engineers have long since observed this critical situation in Hamburg. Within the next decades, a major reconstruction and adaptation
project for Hamburg Central Station is planned, including an extension of platforms and a redesign of the main pedestrian flows. An improvement to the current
situation, however, cannot be expected in the near future, thus alternative measures are required, in anticipation of the development of city's cruise business. In
this regard, cruise tourism has negative impacts on Hamburg, adding to the daily
congestion at the Central Station. According to passenger surveys, 97% of cruise
passengers embarking in Hamburg are residents of a different city, 34% of whom
arrive in the city via the Central Train Station (Inspektour Tourismus- und Regionalentwicklung 2016). This means that during the "peak season" when all cruise
terminals are operating at full capacity, there are an additional 10,000 people passing through the station per day. While placing a significant strain on the city's
transportation network, only 24% of cruise passengers take the initiative to spend
more than two hours in the city itself. This means that the economic benefits of
cruise passenger tourism primarily profit cruise operators and cruise-related business. Tourists report a lack of comfort and orientation upon the very first step of
arrival. A negative first impression gives impetus for visitors to take the first available bus shuttle directly to the cruise terminal (Inspektour Tourismus- und Regionalentwicklung 2016), rather than spending time in the city.
  We contend that a procedural perspective and dynamic form of modelling are
necessary to understand the peculiarities of the Port of Hamburg and its synergies
with the city's socio-economic, functional, and morphological fabric. The multiple
activities of ports—not restricted to cruise operations—will, by way of chain processes, affect entire city operations and urban systems. Ports, as complex systems,
actively integrate multiple procedures and components with regard to individual
actors and the overall structural network (Čišić et al. 2007). In Hamburg, this means
framing the description of port processes beyond the limits of the port itself, and
connecting these, among others, to vital transfer processes happening at the Central Train Station, the central bus terminal, or the airport. It requires a comprehensive solution that defines the multiplicity of individual actors within a structural
network.
  Agent-based models provide a promising tool for visualising and quantifying
critical situations such as the bottleneck at Hamburg Central Station. Additionally,
the models help to improve and optimise chain processes and flows, predicting potential effects of new interventions and planning schemes.

Thus, our long-term vision is to encourage the digitalisation of harbour infrastructures and processes (Brümmerstedt et al. 2017), establishing adequate ABM solutions that model essential port and city processes and interactions. In the short term, however, the aim is to model passenger and luggage transfers linked to cruise tourism—for which the following are necessary: (1) detect and describe, in qualitative terms the spatial pinpoints, hotspots and bottlenecks affecting chained processes and individual passenger comfort; and (2) define, in quantitative terms, the efficiency and performance effects of possible intervention scenarios. The aim is to offer support to decision-makers, by providing new insights for the analysis of the current situation and presenting new port-city process scenarios.

Establishing a Procedural Port-City Model

Process Topology

With a special focus on stakeholder engagement, a series of workshops were held to develop a procedural scheme to depict the routes and modes of transportation taken by passengers when embarking and disembarking. On examining the visualisation of the collected data, a convergence of paths towards the Central Train Station appeared, since the station is also a major node for the transit of regional, long-distance, and airport commuter trains.

The details of this process, as well as the internal chain of activities that passengers follow once inside the cruise terminals, were

Figure 1a: (Below) Representation of different paths from the city to the vessel documented during the workshops.

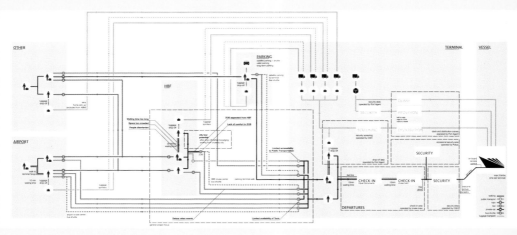

tablished in cooperation with representatives of local cruise op-
ators and the port authority. Finally, the information gathered
uring these workshops was complemented with field observa-
ons and interviews with the ground operators in charge.

1e visualisation of these inputs and findings enabled the docu-
entation of (1) routes and transport modes; (2) chains of events
om the passenger perspective; (3) desired "what if" scenarios,
rther investigated with the developed models. In order to expli-
te linkages between the city's three major cruise terminals and
ban systems, a matrix of existing transportation connections
tween origins and destinations, as integrated into the subse-
uent ABM model, was created.

tablishing the Model

order to visualise and simulate the relational network on a
anular scale, meaning single individual entities, an agent-based
odel was created. This consolidated the process description with
uantitative survey data about cruise passengers, collected by an
ternal research consultancy (Inspektour Tourismus- und Regio-
alentwicklung 2016). These models were enriched by utilising
owd-sourced data, disclosing the activeness of nodes in the
etwork. The function of these external data sources was to
uantify the activeness of places at their initial state, establish-
g the modal split and route choice. To do so, a combination of
1one tracking data, posts gathered from the social media net-
ork Instagram, and a data summary from counting pedestrian
1d vehicle parking records were utilised (Table 1).

Figure 1b: Representation of one
possible path.

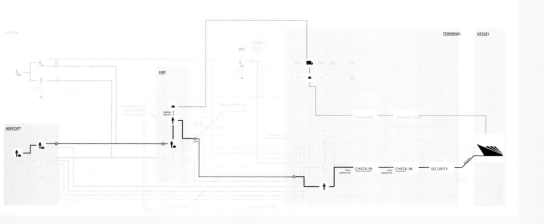

Table 1. Summary of quantitative data sources

Phone tracking: Cruise passengers	Modal split ground / underground / ferry Quantification of people with origin train station Activeness curve of cruise passengers in the train
Instagram: Non-cruise passengers	Route from the train station to cruise terminal followed. Arrival times at the cruise terminal, and length of trip.
Pedestrian counters: Non-cruise passengers	Quantification of people in the train station per day. Probability of flow in pedestrian routes (i.e. surrounding sidewalks and inner corridors)
Terminal parking records: Cruise passengers	Modal split: bus / car / taxi Vehicles arriving and leaving by minute

Phone tracking data were gathered by process of: (1) determining spatial boundaries of the cruise centre; (2) filtering connections to cruise departures by time; (3) detection of users connected to phone towers in departing cruises; (4) tracking back departing cruise passengers to their origin in the city; and (5) selecting users who commenced their trip at the Central Train Station. This process was repeatedly applied for ten different cruise vessels on dates where no extraordinary events occurred in the port (e.g. Hamburg Port Anniversary).

A similar methodology was applied in assessing the retrieved images posted on Instagram which were mainly used to quantify the activeness of non-cruise passengers at the Central Station. To do so, we downloaded a sample of pictures with hashtag or location pins related to either (1) the Central Train Station, or (2) one of the city's three cruise centres: Hamburg Altona, HafenCity, or Steinweders—along with their correlating cruise vessels: *Aida Prima, Aida Perla, MSC Magnifica, MSC Meraviglia,* or *TUI Mein Schiff 4.* These were then filtered according to sources, such as locations and hashtags, with a minimum relevance threshold, of at least 50 pictures, and a time extension of more than one year. This was correlated to posted pictures of users with a presence either at the Central Train Station, or any other location on the same day, assuming potential links to cruise tourism. The remaining sample are sets of pictures posted by people visiting the Central Station with no connection to cruise tourism. Data retrieved from counting pedestrians were used to identify the number of visitors passing through the Central Station each day as well as the most frequented pedestrian routes within the building and the surrounding area. The number of visitors in the station per day was then proportionally distributed to the activity curve of Instagram, by minute, following the most frequent walking paths.

inally, cruise ship terminal parking records were utilised to detail he modal split of passengers arriving at the terminal, using round transportation. Whereas phone tracking data enable a neasurement of the real-time location and route of people, parking records indicate whether groups arrive in one or more shuttle uses or taxis, and the time of day at which they pass through the ruise terminal parking gates.

he gathered data were sufficiently detailed that it was no longer ecessary to model human decision-making at the individual level, apart from simple choices (e.g. passengers queueing in the hortest line). Building a realistic model of complex and unpredictable human cognition and behaviour is a challenging task Bourgais et al. 2018), therefore when there is no necessity for decision-making modelling, the assumption of intentional, simplified ctions is acceptable. Hence, basic triggers—as mutually chained ctions—were defined in the model, instead of modelling comlex human cognitive processes.

, simple, agent-based model representing the current condition f Hamburg's Central Train Station and its urban environment, /as established. The model describes the arrival and departure of assengers, and how the transportation businesses operate the ontinuous routes, connecting the cruise terminals to the station. Vith the model, the socio-spatial behaviours of agents are depicted, evealing critical pinpoints and bottlenecks. These findings are further elaborated and focused on with more precise sub-models.

echnically, the model was designed according to a set of rules nd conditions. The model runs on computed 1-second cycles,

Figure 2: Comparison of temporal activity in Hamburg Central Train Station extracted from Instagram posts (left) and Telecom data tracking, related to passengers travelling on specific vessels (right).

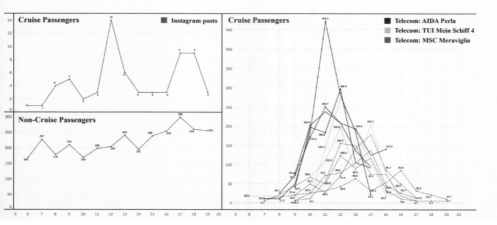

Table 2. Summary of entities utilised

Context	
Environment	Boundaries, Buildings, Walking paths, Road lines, Railways, Cruise terminals
Dynamic Setting	Cars, Subway trains, People in the station
Simulation Agents	
Transportations	Taxis, Bus shuttles, Luggage sprinters
Human Agents	Cruise tourists departing, Cruise tourists arriving, Cruise crew
Entrance Points	Station platforms, Underground station entrances, Taxi stand, Shuttle stop, Sprinter parkings
Exit Points	A general exit point representing cruise cen- tres (outside Central Station boundaries)

restarting the simulation every 36,000 cycles, thus representing the timespan from 8am–6pm. The entities of the model are considered distinct objects, behaving a units and interacting with other entities. State variables are parameters associate with those agents which evolve over time. For this model, the simulation was im plemented by using the software GAMA (Taillandier et al. 2018; Drogoul et al. 201; Grignard et al. 2013), which functions according to the logic that agents form th environment and also determine the spatial setting, in which entities move an behave. Along with agents in a dynamic setting, they constitute the simulatio context in which interactions take place, as explained in Table 2. The context is de scribed spatially, as the environment or urban space; and socially, such as people o the surrounding traffic, which remain constant following the input data describe above. Once the context is set, simulation agents, playing an active role, are de fined—generating information and index measurements. These agents are divide into "human agents" representing people, such as cruise tourists and crew; an "transportation agents" representing vehicles. Entrance and exit points are als considered "active agents". These types of agent represent static places as fixe points in space—such as boarding gates, or entrances—while having an activ function in the simulation, beyond mere spatial representation. They are able t generate other agents. A person arriving at the station is computed as an agen "station platform" creating an agent "cruise tourist", as a bus shuttle arriving at cruise terminal parking would be programmed as an agent "exit point" asking a agent "bus shuttle" to disappear when their location coincides. The definition an integration of this diverse set of agents into one model turned out to be a critica scientific challenge, as there were, thus far, no other reference projects that endeav oured to carry out a in a similar task.

A major challenge in the process of establishing the model was defining the appro priate linkages between agents. Our model postulates that a multitude of simpl processes are connected to each other, in which cruise passengers function as ac on triggers towards other agents. These cruise agents are divided into two groups: those arriving (from the cruise terminal to the Central Train Station) and those departing (from the Central Train Station to the cruise terminal). Cruise passenger agents are modelled by a measure of hourly activity, both in the Central Train Station and in the cruise terminals. This means that a model of arriving and departing passengers—proportional to the number of hourly passengers, as measured in the train station, or the cruise terminals—is generated. Quantifying the passengers who arrive in the train station or the cruise terminals within a range of time effects a concatenation of interactions between agents. This generates a processual visualisation of pinpoints and hotspots, providing a more realistic description than the assumption of a constant inflow independent of variables. Figure 3 illustrates how cruise passengers function as triggers of action with respect to all other agents, taking into account that the data are derived from an external data source. Since cruise passengers are segregated in the act of embarking and disembarking, the processes they trigger are represented separately. However, the model simulates both embarking and disembarking processes simultaneously. In terms of visualisation, the model simultaneously functions at two

Figure 3: Visualisation of the model working at two scales.

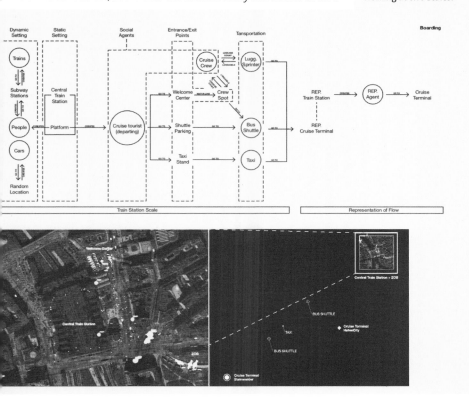

scales, representing: (1) spatial movements (e.g. people and cars moving along the streets); and (2) city-wide, multimodal flow transitions, without specific spatial movements but statistical descriptions (e.g. buses departing from the train station and arriving at the cruise terminal). Both scales are linked, as shown on the left and right sides of Figure 3. This cross-scale procedural description—established by the project team to derive a valid ABM—proved to be a highly valuable asset for the port and cruise-related stakeholders, since it is the first adequate process description of the Port of Hamburg to date.

Data Extraction and Interpretation of Results

The models, devised in accordance with the described methods and procedures were applied with first test runs, to simulate different scenarios of chain processes and spatial interventions. The data extracted from these test runs provided insight into tentative interpretations of results. As previously stated, a critical factor at the beginning of the embarkation process is the degree of disorientation which passengers experience as they move within the Central Train Station (Inspektour Tourismus- und Regionalentwicklung 2016).

Passengers claim that it is unclear where the Welcome Centre, situated at *Hachmanplatz*, on the north-east corner of the station's building, is located. In this sense, the ABM paid special attention to environmental perception. It gave the passenger-agents "knowledge" of where to go, when a clear visual connection to the Welcome Centre was established, or when they could interact with other agents with "knowledge" of the centre's location. As it turned out, time spent in disoriented movement varies markedly, depending on the direction which the passenger-agent takes at the initial step. Those going east, for example, establish a connection with the Welcome Centre within only 250 cycles; while those going west need 700 cycles. The amount of time passengers spent disoriented depends on knowing the location of the target destination, and is therefore determined by the initial direction passengers chose to turn in the station. This suggests that a simple intervention, for example the placement of information signs inside the station building pointing towards the Welcome Centre may significantly optimise passenger transfer.

In addition, further bottlenecks appear (Inspektour Tourismus- und Regionalentwicklung 2016) during (1) the drop-off process at the Welcome Centre, since passenger arrival times vary, subject to train schedules and peak hours; and (2) boarding of the bus shuttles (although to a lesser extent). The indicator of time expense, as it relates to the second bottleneck, remained constant in all tested scenarios, since the process of getting inside a bus remains virtually unaffected by improvements in design. However, a variation of the number of crew members serving the check-in process, inversely influenced the waiting time during peak hours. A critical point, when the queue at the Welcome Centre reaches the building of the rain station, occurs in of peak hours scenario, when, for example, arge vessels (holding more than 4,000 passengers) arrive at the ort.

During the preliminary workshops, walking distance between the Welcome Centre and the bus shuttles was another focal point. In his case, orientation was not a difficulty for passengers once they ad dropped off their luggage at the Welcome Centre. However, he distance to the bus shuttles is significant, requiring passen- ers to walk about 500 metres. A shared observation expressed uring the workshop sessions was that passengers would be likely o subsequently perform the actions of (1) dropping off their lug- age, and then (2) walking directly to the bus shuttle, meaning hat passengers usually drop off their luggage and walk "auto- natically" to the bus shuttle without wandering around the city, topping for a coffee or engaging in leisure or consumption activ- .ies. As the ABM simulation depicted, the effect of this phenome- on is that the bottleneck caused by the Welcome Centre's lug- age drop-off is reproduced—albeit, on a smaller scale—when aking the bus shuttle.

.s expected, the different intervention scenarios had a clear effect n movement flows and waiting times. The planned intervention vithin the Central Train Station will increase the capacity of the Welcome Centre, and move the bus shuttles closer—thus ad- ressing the two largest bottlenecks. Overall efficiency will be in- reased with a direct intervention that focuses on the bottlenecks, ringing reduced waiting times and significantly shortened ueues. As Figure 4 illustrates, a visual comparison of the differ- nt scenarios clearly shows the increase in efficiency.

Figure 4: Comparison of results (Y = amount of people, X = time) in different scenarios tested.

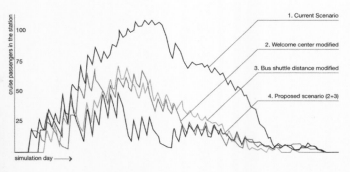

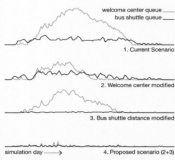

Conclusions and Outlook

It was possible to create a first, tentative, agent-based model that is able to simu late and describe the positive impact and possibilities of various alternative sce narios. Although the input data were aggregated and extrapolated from statistic bearing segmentation, it was possible to quantify the impact of the scenario-pro posals for a comparison to the current situation. Also, a conceptual process o pre-simulation was validated, to be applied prior to the actual decision-making. I regards to the multimodal land transportation of Hamburg's cruise tourism, th modifications, as tested within the different scenarios, are expected to enhance th comfort and satisfaction of cruise transfers; raising the efficiency of the chain-pro cesses to the benefit of both tourists and stakeholders. Therefore, the model lend itself to supporting the early stages of discussions and deliberations around urba planning and decision-making. That said, nevertheless it continues to require fu ther development, based on refined data input and self-learning from output.

The more refined the input data, the more reliable the model and simulation ar expected to be. Skilful cross-referencing of location and behavioural data, com bined with a historic and socio-economic understanding of cruise providers, route and seasons, extened the possibilities for predicting flows of people, as related t multimodal transportation connecting incoming vessels. This has the added poten tial to affect the socio-economic behaviour of cruise passengers in the wider urba context. Investigating alternative scenarios was defined in advance by externa agents, such as in the preliminary workshops. Instead of testing specific, pre-select ed scenarios, stochastic machine-learning techniques linked to processes of batc simulation empowered the model to recommend specific modifications in specifi circumstances. In addition to sharpening the input data, these techniques allowe a more flexible adaptation of parameters for every case study, thus improving th simulation power of the overall approach. A scaling up of the approach tested i this research enhances the Digital Urban Twin model to include additional hu man-centric data (e.g. lifestyle and activities) in order to systematically address cru cial challenges of the global urban age—generating knowledge by exploring, visu alising, and testing.

References

onso, L., Y.R. Zhang, A. Grignard, A. Noyman, Y. Sakai, M. ElKatsha, R. Doorley, and K. Larson (2018). "Cityscope: a data-driven interactive simulation tool for urban design. Use case Volpe." *International conference on complex systems*: pp. 253–261. Cham.

AA (2011). *World Port Rankings*, viewed 12 March 2019, http://aapa.files.cms-plus.com/PDFs/WORLD%20PORT%20RANKINGS%202011.pdf.

urgais, M., P. Taillandier, L. Vercouter, and C. Adam (2018). "Emotion modeling in social simulation: A survey." *Journal of Artificial Societies and Social Simulation* 21.02.

wen D. and J. Clarke (2002). "Reflections on tourist satisfaction research: Past, present and future." *Journal of Vacation Marketing* 8.4: pp. 297–308.

ümmerstedt, K., R. Fiedler, V. Flitsch, C. Jahn, H. Roreger, B. Sarpong, S. Saxe, and B. Scharfenberg (2017). *Digitalization of Seaports—Visions of the Future*. Hamburg.

šić D. , P. Komadina, and B. Hlača (2007). "Network analysis of the mediterranean port supply chain structures." *Pomorstvo* 21.01: pp. 211–220.

ogoul, A., E. Amouroux, P. Caillou, B. Gaudou, A. Grignard, N. Marilleau, P. Taillandier, M. Vavasseur, D.A. Vo, and J. D. Zucker (2013). "Gama: multi-level and complex environment for agent-based models and simulations." *12th International Conference on Autonomous agents and multi-agent systems*: pp. 1361–1362.

ignard, A. N. Macià, L. Alonso Pastor, A. Noyman, Y. Zhang, and K. Larson (2018). "Cityscope andorra: a multi-level interactive and tangible agent-based visualization." *Proceedings of the 17th International Conference on Autonomous Agents and MultiAgent Systems*: pp. 1939–1940.

ignard, A., P. Taillandier, B. Gaudou, D.A. Vo, N.Q Huynh, and A. Drogoul (2013). "GAMA 1.6: Advancing the art of complex agent-based modeling and simulation." *International conference on principles and practice of multi-agent systems*: pp. 117–131. Berlin, Heidelberg.

A (2019). *Hafen Hamburg*, viewed 11 March 2019, https://www.hafen-hamburg.de/en/cruise.

spektour (2016). Tourismus- und Regionalentwicklung. KREUZFAHRTPASSAGIER- UND CREWBEFRAGUNG. Report.

erk, O., and M. Hesse (2012). The competitiveness of global port-cities: The case of Hamburg, Germany. *OECD Regional Development Working Papers*. 2012/06.

guyen-Huu, T., W. Gruel, and K. Larson (2018). "The Impact of New Mobility Modes on a City: A Generic Approach Using ABM." *Unifying Themes in Complex Systems IX: Proceedings of the Ninth International Conference on Complex Systems*. Cham.

yman, A. (2015). *POWERSTRUCTURES: the urban form of regulations*. (Dissertation) Massachusetts.

oyman, A., T. Holtz, J. Kröger, J.R. Noennig, and K. Larson (2017). "Finding places: HCI platform for public participation in refugees' accommodation process." *Procedia computer science* 112: pp. 2463–2472.

hirmar S. (2018). *Ankunft in zwölf Jahren*, viewed 19 March 2019, https://www.zeit.de/2018/35/hamburg-hauptbahnhof-ausbau-verkehr-probleme.

illandier, P., B. Grignard, Q.N. Huynh, N. Marilleau, P. Caillou, D. Philippon, and A. Drogoul (2018). "Building, composing and experimenting complex spatial models with the GAMA platform." *GeoInformatica* 23.02: pp. 299–322.

ggelas, G. K., and I. N. Lagoudis (2010). "Analysing the supply chain strategy of the cruise industry: the case of a small cruise company". *International Association of Maritime Economists*. Lisbon.

en, J.F. Leurent, and X.A. Xie (2017). "Transit Bottleneck Model for Optimal Control Strategies and its Use in Traffic Assignment in Paris." *Transportation research procedia* 22: pp. 65–74.

3. Grassroots Participatory Mapping for Geospatial Database Enhancement with e-Planning in Sri Lanka

GPTS Hemakumara

Abstract

Sri Lanka's administrative structure is made up of nine provinces, which are subd
vided into twenty-five districts; the districts are further subdivided into 231 Distri
Secretariat (DS) divisions, which are in turn broken down into 14,022 Grama Nila
hari (GN) divisions. Confusion prevails regarding the many different, and cons
quently overlapping, administrative boundaries of the various departments. Als
boundary marking errors proliferate alongside a lack of clear information abou
geopolitical demarcations. Therefore, there is an urgent need for the precise tra
ing and redrawing of administrative boundaries. For this, the digital geospatial d
tabase must be enhanced, since it is necessary for achieving adequate e-Plannin
in Sri Lanka. As a first step, this study discusses the errors in Sri Lanka's boundar

emarcations of GN divisions. Next, suggestions for correcting the
oundary errors are offered. Improving the GIS database by incor-
orating grassroots information on housing boundaries is the
rincipal recommendation of the research. In 2018, Sri Lanka had
,022 GN divisions, and 5,905,574 housing units in 2012, meaning,
at there is an average of 428 houses per GN division. Correcting
e GN boundaries, generating digital maps of housing units and
aking census blocks is therefore only possible with public partic-
ation. This study focuses on three mapping pilot projects which
volve public input. As a result of the first pilot survey, the exist-
g boundaries of GN divisions were successfully corrected with
e participation of GN officers and the public. The second pilot
udy focused on locating all the houses and entering the data on
digital information system within a GN division that comprised
sample of 250 houses. The third and final pilot study developed a
ousing unit information system which covered 50 parameters
ch as social, economic and environmental data and in particu-
r housing with a sample size of 500 units so as to facilitate
Planning and statistical analysis. This grassroots geospatial in-
rmation system will contribute significantly to the establish-
ent of an effective e-Planning system in Sri Lanka.

eywords: E-Planning, Geospatial, GIS Mapping, Public Participa-
on, Urban Planning.

troduction

lministrative boundaries are essential for effective governance
ld to serve semi-autonomous units. Government decisions are
utinely taken across the country on various matters, such as, for
:ample , the provision of infrastructural facilities, subsistence al-
wances, enforcement of rules and regulations, allocation of for-
gn aid, and welfare programmes. Clearly defined boundaries are
ecessary in order that all these decisions can target specific ar-
ls. Standard administration units in Sri Lanka consist of nine
ovinces, twenty-five districts, 332 DS divisions, and 14,022 GN di-
sions. Administrative boundaries serve census and electoral
irposes, among others, and delineate other areas of jurisdiction
 Sri Lanka, such as law enforcement, the remit of the Medical
fficer of Health (MoH), judiciary, education, and so forth. Hence,
is necessary to superimpose boundaries from GNs, Sub Districts
SD), Districts, Provinces and National government to allow a

bottom up approach. The current boundaries, however, are not accurately mapped t
reflect the terrain's existing, ground-level layout and man-made features (Dayaratn
2010). Therefore, this study attempts to compile an accurate grassroots GN data
base with the assistance of the public and other stakeholders.

The majority of GN boundaries are demarcated along social, economic, linguistic, o
physical lines. Social boundaries may occur wherever social differences lead to ur
equal access to resources and opportunities (Nast and Blokland 2014). These issue
may be affected by factors such as race, gender, religion, and physical capacity. I
some places, for example, women are not allowed to perform specific jobs or trav
in certain areas. Moreover, economic boundaries segregate people with differer
incomes or levels of prosperity. In certain instances, these boundaries correspond t
national borders. Areas rich in resources such as crude oil or minerals are more like
ly to be prosperous, while people who live in areas without any significant resour
es stay poor. People are also willing to pay more to live in areas that have access t
natural or economic resources, such as beautiful views, excellent schools, hospital
and convenient shopping facilities (Lamont et al. 2014). Further, linguistic boundar
create divisions in areas where people speak different languages. Physical bounda
ies, on the other hand, are the most obvious type of boundaries, represented by
naturally occurring barrier between two areas. Rivers, mountain ranges, ocean
and deserts are examples of physical boundaries. Rivers may serve as a commo
boundary between countries—and between provinces within a country (Gunara
na 2006).

Public participation is a fundamental aspect of making adequate adjustments t
the existing Geographic Information System (GIS) digital mapping databases at di
ferent levels (Liverman 1998). Accordingly, this study focuses on three case studie
as pilot surveys for building an adequate grassroots GIS database, with the objec
tive of enhancing e-Planning techniques in Sri Lanka.

Problem Statement
Grassroots mapping and the compiled digital database are critical elements for th
implementation of e-Planning in Sri Lanka. However, at present, the Sri Lanka vi
lage-level database has several spatial, technical, and demarcation shortcoming
In sum, these issues pose a significant obstacle to the effective and accurate imple
mentation of e-Planning in Sri Lanka. Therefore, there is a pressing need for a qua
itative, grassroots geospatial GIS mapping system. This study discusses several neg
ative factors that lower the value and usefulness of the existing GN database in S
Lanka. The study applies the expertise of relevant stakeholders, together with view
and knowledge from the public, as necessary components of a grassroots databas
in order to enhance the geospatial mapping process in Sri Lanka.

Methodology

The methodology of the participatory approach to grassroots mapping in Sri Lanka can be divided into three phases, as shown in Table 1. The focus of this study is building an accurate, grassroots mapping system in collaboration with local communities. These methods were implemented in three pilot surveys conducted from 2007–2015 in the Western Province of Sri Lanka.

Table 1: Existing Information and Sample				
Phase	**Total Size**	**Research Method**	**Sample Size**	**Stakeholders**
Correction of existing GN boundaries	14,022	Pilot survey	3 GN Divs.	Village leaders, GN officers, GIS technicians
Development of housing locations and basic data in GN areas	6 Million	Pilot survey	250 Houses	Villagers, GPS and GIS technicians
Development of housing units' boundaries	Approx. 5 Million	Pilot survey	500 Houses	Villagers, village leaders, GIS technicians, town planners

All three case studies were supplied with relevant GIS data at grassroots level after holding consultations with public officials and other relevant officers. Difficulties and obstacles were highlighted, and helpful recommendations made.

Discussion

Case Study 1: Rectification of GN Boundaries in Sri Lanka

The rectification of incorrect GN boundaries in Sri Lanka is a massive and difficult task, as highlighted in Figure 1. The project began in 2007 with the initial pilot survey, in the Kalutara DS division of Kalutara District. Demarcation of correct GN boundaries is time-consuming, and the presence of GN officers is essential throughout the entire mapping process. Since most of the relevant GN boundary lines are on real ground, they can only be tracked by the existing system, requiring the presence of the area's GN officer.

Figure 1: Difficulties faced in correcting GN boundaries in the field

d. Shrubs

a. Various private premises

b. Rough surfaces

c. Inaccessible terrain

Figure 2 depicts the maps of the three GN divisions corrected during the pilot survey, based on the newly acquired information and data. Sri Lanka has approximately 14,022 GN divisions, for most of which the boundaries, had been inaccurately surveyed. It is therefore necessary to correct them in cooperation with the relevant authorities, such as the Department of Census and Statistics, the Survey Department of Sri Lanka, the Urban Development Authority, and the Divisional Secretariat Divisions, along with village leaders.

Figure 2: Corrected GN boundary

a. GPS tracking files

b. Existing and corrected boundaries

ase Study 2: Development of Housing Units in Geospatial atabase of GN Areas

gure 3 depicts the procedures for generating a database of all ousing units in a particular GN area. The initial project was con- ucted as a pilot case study in the *Kosgama* 480A GN division of e *Hanwella* DS division in collaboration with the Urban Devel- ment Authority (UDA) of Sri Lanka. Housing unit data were nked with annual electoral registration information, as collected the Elections Department. The second step of the extensive ork of grassroots mapping is plotting the estimated 6 million uses located within the 14,022 GN divisions, in order to make ore effective e-Planning possible in the future. Figure 3 presents e database of just one of the 14,022 GN divisions.

Figure 3: Development of housing units in the geospatial database of GN areas

Source: Data file prepared by Hemakumara

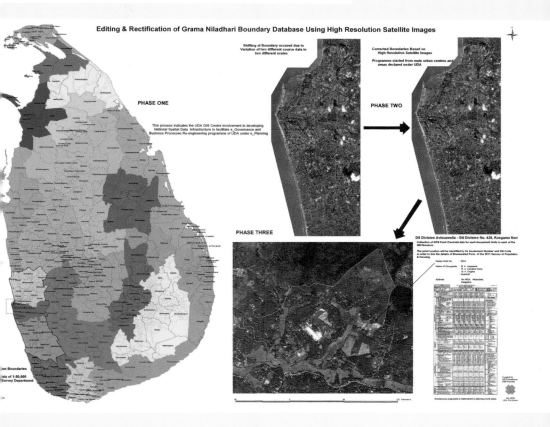

Case Study 3: Concept of Public Participatory Mapping for the Demarcation of Housing Land Plots

Sample Size
In order adequately to document the housing plots of one GN division, the entire population sample of the two villages of; Karunagama and Paranawatta was taken. Accordingly, interviews were conducted in each household within the study area, which included about 454 houses, as shown in Figure 4.

Figure 4: Stable house (A) and unstable house (B) in the study area

Method of Interview
Three trained interviewers administered the questionnaires over the course of two months. All interviewers were community leaders who had previously received training in data collection from the Department of Census and Statistics. They were all residents of the same village, well known to the house owners, and within the wider locality. Usually about 20–30 plot owners per week were interviewed. Interviewers held weekly meetings in the field, and their performance was randomly evaluated. The data were then computed with supportive GIS mapping on the same day consultations were held with local people (Martella et al. 1999).

Linking the Field Data with GIS
As illustrated in Figure 5, data from 454 household addresses and their plot boundaries were entered into the GIS system. However, the most challenging task was collecting primary data of socioeconomic, behavioural, and geospatial details in relation to every household in the study area (Kumar 2010). For this, face-to-face in

rviews with questionnaires were conducted with households
overing the core study area. By means of SPSS, all household in-
ormation was processed. The SPSS results, including the value of
ach household, were then combined with an attribute table of
rc GIS 10, and entered into the land plot maps (Hossain et al.
009). The land plot of individual households defines the unit of
nalysis, necessitating the participation of the public to obtain
e spatial details of land plots (Kwan 2000). In the case of the
rid, or cell-based analysis, this is done by sampling the validity of
round information using automation modelling (Matthews et
. 2007). In this study, several discussions were held with individ-
al households, along with meetings at the relevant sites. Follow-
g vector-based GIS analysis, the plot locations were marked on
e map, as shown in Figure 5.

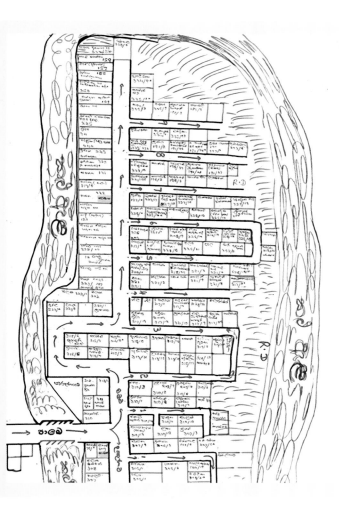

Figure 5: Example of public
participation-based land plot
mapping in the study area

Geo-Spatial Information System for Housing Plots

Since information concerning the demarcation of land plots wa
obtained from public opinion and knowledge, it was necessary t
verify its validity through high-resolution images (Liu and Yan
2015). Satellite images were geo-referenced with local coordinat
values, and by techniques of screen digitisation land parcels (plot
of the entire study area were digitised. Then, all relevant variable
were tabulated into a GIS attribute table and marked on the ma
as shown in Figure 6, and its related information in Table 2 below

Figure 6: Geospatial database of the
study area

ndings, Highlights, and Implementation
rocess of Grassroots Mapping

hree case studies were separately conducted at different times.
he extrapolated findings are useful for streamlining existing
rassroots mapping development, which the research suggests
hould be undertaken at the national level.

Table 2: Attribute information of Figure 6

able   □
|~|·|믾·|멺멻 ▣ 쀼 ✕

ouseholds

FID	Shape *	R_NAME	HOUSE_NUMB	NUM_FAMILY	MALE	FEMALE	NUM_FAMILI	FAMILY_TYP	HHH_INCOME	FAMILY_INC	F_INC	F_EXPENDI	F_SAVING
299	Point	B A Devika	315_13_1	3	2	1	1	3	18000	18000	18	15500	2500
300	Point	S Ravendra	317_13	4	2	2	1	3	20000	30000	30	22000	8000
301	Point	R Shashi Latha	315_16	2	1	1	1	2	20000	26000	26	14000	12000
302	Point	R Amara	315_11	4	2	2	1	3	20000	30000	30	20000	10000
303	Point	G K Manuasha Sadamal	317_8_B	4	2	2	1	3	20000	25000	25	23000	2000
304	Point	Valu Nandani	317_9	5	2	3	1	3	18000	18000	18	17500	500
305	Point	H M Nandawathi	121_334	4	2	2	1	3	20000	26000	26	24000	2000
306	Point	Edga (Filip Emma)	345	3	1	2	1	3	16000	16000	16	14000	2000
307	Point	Harshani (Podinona Duwa)	335_4	3	2	1	1	3	18000	18000	18	13000	5000
308	Point	G D Suwarna Kanthi	335_8A	4	2	2	1	3	15000	15000	15	14000	1000
309	Point	Podinona	195	5	2	3	1	3	16000	16000	16	15000	1000
310	Point	A S SelvaKumari (Rumesh)	108_8	2	1	1	1	2	13000	13000	13	12000	1000
311	Point	K Selvadori (Suresh)	306_10	4	3	1	1	4	15000	25000	25	22000	3000
312	Point	Biso Manike	305	2	1	1	1	6	8000	20000	20	12000	8000
313	Point	Shiromi AanDias	305_3	6	4	2	1	3	20000	20000	20	19000	1000
314	Point	Pulmoli Chanchala / Nishan	315_3	5	1	4	1	3	22000	22000	22	20000	2000

Table 3: Conclusion Summary of Three Mapping Pilot Projects

Task Level	Summary
Task 1: GN level boundary correction	Considerable disparities are noticed in all three of the surveyed GN areas. The cost of accurately mapping one GN boundary is esti-mated at between Rs.10,000–50,000. Presently, no surveyed GN boundaries in Sri Lanka are 100% correct. Training is required for local officers to mark the GN bounda-ries correctly with public participation. The cooperation of GN officers and village leaders is essenti-al in order to demarcate the GN division boundary. An accurate geospatial database of GN boundaries will form the foundation of the e-Planning process in Sri Lanka.
Task 2: Develop a Housing Singl: Database	Google Earth and open-source mapping software techniques are used to locate houses precisely. GPS surveys are desirable, but not always applicable. GN officers and village leaders are needed to iden-tify all the houses within the GN division. The DSD office plays a crucial role in this process. This database is linked to the existing electoral database. The task can only be implemented after the other tasks are completed. The approximate cost will be Rs. 50,000 per GN unit.
Task 3: Housing unit land plots / census blocks	Information from residents in the relevant area is essential to de-marcate the units of analysis and housing plots. All information about the land plots is collected by a questionnaire. Task 1 and Task 2 of this study must be accomplished first. Based on spatial information and survey information on housing clusters, census blocks are identified, which will facilitate buil-ding the next layer of grassroots-mapping in Sri Lanka. Research cost per GN unit will be Rs.50,000 to complete the GIS database and survey.

This study can be introduced to local authorities in the Colombo Metropolitan Region (CMR) as the Geospatial Household Management System. The local authority annually allocates funds for various activities, such as for the prevention of dengue disease, and for infrastructural needs. Practical programmes making use of these research findings could be established and financed with existing funds. For example, the following activities could be commenced: training local authorities to conduct surveys on houses and housing conditions within their areas of purview; running a public awareness programme for recognising emerging health and environmental issues; instituting a Housing Information Database as part of a national e-Planning system, maintained by a technical support team and annually updated by local authorities; relocating low-income housing occupants to localities that offer better livelihood opportunities; ensuring the systematic rehabilitation of housing in under-served areas and of a land reform plan for the removal of houses with minimal disruption to occupants' lives.

Conclusion
In order to facilitate e-Planning in Sri Lanka, a grassroots participatory mapping for improving the geo-spatial database remains in the development stage. Discussions continue about the specific tasks it is expected to perform. Three case studies generated a mapping of housing and a survey of boundaries. The above three steps are essential for achieving this objective. These case studies are interconnected with each other, and with the e-Planning system. The study provides an indication of the scope of work and of the scale of the task that lie ahead. It also gives indication as to the ways and means by which the objectives can be achieved while providing an estimate of the financial commitments based on the knowledge gained by surveying three cases. The study was conducted at the GN-DSD-District-Provincial level (Bottom to Top Levels). Highlighted throughout the three case studies is the fact that public consultation was the major component of the grassroots mapping process. Conducting accurate mapping on the ground, was key to the research as spatial planning activities are a means of implementing e-Planning. Therefore, it is strongly recommended that affected authorities adopt and implement the same survey methods used in the study, affecting the gradual transition to successful e-Planning in Sri Lanka.

References

ayaratne R. (2010). "Moderating urbanization and managing growth: How can Colombo prevent the emerging chaos?" *Working paper//World Institute for Development Economics Research.*

unaratna K.L. (2006). *Spatial Concerns in Development: A Sri Lankan Perspective.* New Delhi.

ossain, M., S. Chowdhury, N. Das, et al. (2009). "Integration of GIS and multicriteria decision analysis for urban aquaculture development in Bangladesh." *Landscape and Urban Planning* 90: pp 119–133.

umar, R. (2010). *Research methodology: A step-by-step guide for beginners.* Thousand Oaks.

wan, M.P. (2000). "Analysis of human spatial behaviour in a GIS environment: Recent developments and future prospects." *Journal of Geographical Systems* 2: pp. 85–90.

amont, M., S. Beljean, and M. Clair (2014). "What is missing? Cultural processes and causal pathways to inequality." *Socio-Economic Review* 12: pp. 573–608.

u, T. and X. Yang (2015). "Monitoring land changes in an urban area using satellite imagery, GIS and landscape metrics." *Applied Geography* 56: pp. 42–54.

verman, D.M. (1998). *People and pixels: Linking remote sensing and social science.* National Academies Press.

Martella, R.C., R. Nelson and N.E. Marchand-Martella (1999). *Research methods.* Boston, MA.

Matthews, R., N. Gilbert, A. Roach et al. (2007). "Agent-based land-use models: a review of applications." *Landscape Ecology* 22.14: pp. 47–59.

ast, J. and T. Blokland (2014). "Social mix revisited: Neighbourhood institutions as setting for boundary work and social capital." *Sociology* 48: pp. 482–499.

4. Curating Cultural Data for Cities: In Conversation with Vishal Kumar

Vanessa Weber/Vishal Kumar

Inspired by contemporary transformations of culture in cities and by scientific advancements for gaining insight into different types of data, this conversation explores the practices and challenges of curating cultural data. The dialogue began at the 'Art Without Humans' workshop at City Science Summit 2019, and exchange continued via email until March 2020. This contribution depicts research approaches designed to illuminate how urban situations are translated into digital representations (e.g. data sets, visualisations) and how these digital representations in turn shape urban realities. Here the cultural data scientist Vishal Kumar, who investigates exploratory practices of curating cultural data in cities with digital tools, discusses his work, elaborating on the increasing importance of curating data-related practices in urban situations. Traditionally, curation is a practice associated with the arts: the term commonly refers to the process of collecting, sorting, and mediating works of art in spaces such as museums or galleries. Over the past few years, however, the notion of curating has expanded and resonated as a methodology and practice in disciplines beyond the arts. In this conversation, Vishal Kumar outlines the new challenges of *datafied* urban life and explains how knowledge gained from cultural data has led to practices of curating such data for cities, contributing to the creation of urban culture.

anessa Weber (VW): Curatorial practices, customary in the art
world for purposes of collecting, sorting, and mediating, have expanded to a diversity of other cultural fields. With the rise of
technology-enabled networks, particularly with the ubiquitous
use of the internet, curatorial practices are omnipresent, from
the curation of reading lists and online blogs to Instagram pro-
les, and so on (Rosenbaum 2011). Practices of content curation
are found in various aspects of cultural life — everywhere data
are collected, sorted, and mediated to be shared with a broad au-
ience. In light of the expansion of curatorial practices, a shift in
the conditions and mechanisms determining the production of
rban culture and its societal impact becomes evident. The cul-
ural scientist Jeremy Morris describes 'Curation by Code' (2015),
or example, as when automated recommendation systems in
music services determine the experience of music content the
udience receives, thereby shaping trends and cultures. New
technologies and data production are affecting society and par-
cularly contemporary urban life. Vishal, against this back-
round, how can cultural data be described, and from what
ources do they stem?

Vishal Kuma (VK): Put simply, cultural data are any data related to
the arts, humanities, and cultural studies. For a holistic understanding, though, several categories for dividing and segmenting
cultural data are useful. There are various typologies of cultural
data, whether qualitative or quantitative — such as, for example,
textual, image, video, audio, numeric or spatial, all of which may,
further, be either structured or unstructured.

The academic Lev Manovich coined the concept of 'cultural analytics' in 2007, making two helpful distinctions concerning cultural
data. On the one hand, data generated in the digital humanities
include traditional cultural heritage and artefacts, and the digitisation of museum and collections — all of which may be composed of
visual and textual data. As Manovich (2017, p. 259) points out, 'The
very first project to digitise cultural texts and make them freely
available was Project Gutenberg', which started in 1970. Manovich
describes these texts as historical-cultural data sets. On the other
hand, data generated by social computing are understood as 'computer science research that analyses content and activity on social
networks' (Manovich 2016, p. 3). These data, generated from 'activity
on the most popular social networks (Flickr, Instagram, YouTube,

Twitter, etc.), user-created content shared on these network (tweets, images, video, etc.), and also users' interactions with th content (likes, favorites, reports, comments) (Manovich 2016, p. 2 are described as contemporary cultural data sets.

Spatial data related to art and culture are included in these tw sets of cultural data. These data comprise, for example, the locatio of cultural buildings, public spaces, or objects in a geographic coo dinate system, interlaced with useful attributes about building spaces, or objects. A relevant example is the *Cultural Infrastructur Map* introduced by the mayor of London in 2019, which for the firs time plots — effectively, curates — the locations of cultural infra structures throughout the city of London, revealing it alongsid spatial data of transportation networks and population growt Another example is data for points of interest from Google Place as components of Google Maps Platform, Foursquare, or Yelp. Fu ther spatial data include telecommunication and network data co lected from GPS and Wi-Fi signals at expansive cultural events, m seums, or public areas. In addition, socio-economic data related t art and culture are included. Arts Council England, a gover ment-funded body dedicated to promoting the performing, visu and literary arts, annually make requests for pertinent econom data from cultural institutions. This information is then processe curated, and published on their website or the national gover ment's website.

Moreover, the Cultural Data Project in the United States collects d tailed information on various indicators about cultural institutior such as revenues and expenses; marketing activities; investmen and loans; attendance and pricing; and staffing and volunteers. Su veys conducted by cultural institutions and governments are an a ditional source of useful cultural data. The Taking Part Survey[1] in th United Kingdom is a fantastic example of the collection of data c engagements in the arts, museums and galleries, archives, librarie heritage, and sports. Finally, it is worth highlighting the prevalenc of open-source data from public city portals as an emerging sourc of cultural data. Online platforms such as data.world[2] contain fc ty-six separate cultural data sets, mostly from North American inst tutions, including the District of Columbia and the City of New Yor Furthermore, the Australian government has a web portal calle Cultural Data Online[3], which provides access to a broad range of r search relating to the arts and culture in Australia.

1 https://www.gov.uk/ guidance/taking-part-survey

2 https://data.world/datasets/cultural

3 https://www.arts.gov.au/ mcm/cultural-data-online

(VW): You note that cultural data evolving from various sources and produced for different purposes are worthy of data analysis. When considering curatorial practices within the field of urban cultural data, we may return to the aspect of collecting, sorting, and mediating that data. The cultural scientists Mikkel Flyverbom and John Murray (2018) analyse processes related to what they call *datastructuring*. They elaborate on the production and processing of data as social activities, whereby the processes of collecting and sorting play a significant role, and they point out that 'we still know relatively little about the moderation and curation practices of social media platforms at the level of datastructuring' (Flyverbom & Murray 2018, p. 10). How is it possible to gain insight into cultural data? Which digital tools do you use? And how do these relate to curatorial practices?

(K): For my work, I generally use a wide variety of data sources, but the main categories include urban, social media, survey, and economic data. For a recent academic study, I measured the economic impact and value of cultural infrastructure on local neighbourhoods in London by means of geographically weighted regression models, using an estimated 80,000 Airbnb listings as proxies for supply and demand of local neighbourhoods in London. Then I applied about 8,000 cultural venues and a range of socioeconomic data as dependent variables. From that study, I can say that an excellent resource for measuring culture in urban areas is the European Commission's *Cultural and Creative Cities Monitor*, which gathers twenty-nine indicators for 168 cities in thirty European countries.

My academic research aims to utilise cultural data for measuring the socioeconomic impact and value of art and culture in cities. The methods and tools are a combination of data science and visualisation; machine learning and computer vision; urban economics and statistics; and social media analytics. Typically I research large-scale citywide cultural events and policies, but I do sometimes include local one-off events and museum exhibitions. Also, I am increasingly interested in agent-based modelling and simulations. My research relates to curatorial practices in that I collect, sort, and clean cultural data, making it suitable for analysis or machine learning.

Then I utilise my background as a cultural data scientist to argue for sustained investment in art and culture, in pursuit of influencing policy and market dynamics. For instance, when I was leading the data science research for the first *London Borough of Culture* initiative in 2019, I analysed over 50,000 social media posts and 3,000 surveys related to the twelve-month programme. I used natural language processing and machine-learning techniques to unearth how audiences responded to events. When we controlled for demographics, we found that certain events create more positive social reactions. These data were included in a final evaluation document by the Insights and Evaluation team at Waltham Forest Council, when they argued for the benefits of art and culture to policy-makers at the mayor of London's office. Moreover, I consulted with the Coventry City of Culture Trust to devise a citywide data plan for optimising all data generated as part of the UK's next City of Culture in 2021. That data plan document was used for discussions with city officials and urban planners to make the case for increased investment in data systems for art and culture. In addition, the Trust has a Technical Reference Group where I sit alongside colleagues from the government, think-tanks, and cultural institutions to help devise new methodologies for analysing and researching the impact of cultural policy.

It's very useful to work on current cultural policy projects like these because these institutions create and curate robust frameworks for evaluation. Working as a consultant on citywide cultural projects necessitates curating and connecting entire systems of information by data canals, so that data can easily flow into data lakes or data reservoirs, so to speak. Working in real-world contexts, outside academia, further expands my understanding of local versus cloud-based computing systems, and the importance of their interaction. Think of it like an orchestra!

(VW): You describe yourself as a cultural data scientist, using cultural data to gain insights into the dynamics of culture and then influence policy-making based on data interaction and information design. Dominant narratives contend that the vast amount of data generated in the urban realm will allow insight into all aspects of urban life. However, urban data are often static data sets that are sourced and translated into maps or statistics. With this in mind, how can dynamics of culture—described as ephemeral and fluid—be processed by the use of cultural data, and how can valid scientific insights be derived from data that attempts to translate ephemeral phenomena into static objects? In other words, what

oes cultural data science mean, and how can it contribute to un-
erstanding the dynamics of urban culture?

(VK): The best way to explain what cultural data science means is by explaining what it does not mean. Cultural data science is not cultural analytics, much like data science is not data analytics. The nuance is very subtle, perhaps a matter of semantics, but there is a difference. The first hurdle is understanding the dichotomy between 'data analytics' and 'data science'—which in itself is quite tricky. Data analytics is often referred to as a 'process' or 'procedure' that transforms raw data into meaningful information in order to discern patterns (Power et al. 2018). By contrast, data science—a term that still lacks consensus (Irizarry 2020—has its roots in academia and is often referred to as a 'discipline' or a 'study' to 'extract knowledge from information' (Dhar 2013). Data science unifies 'statistics, data analysis, machine learning and their related methods' (Hayashi 1996) to question and test hypotheses with data by writing algorithms and building statistical models. A publication in the *Harvard Data Science Review* written by Meng (2019) explains that data science is 'best understood as a collection of disciplines with complementary foundations, perspectives, approaches, and aims, but with a shared grand mission'. Furthermore, Irizarry (2020) extends Meng's (2019) definition to describe data science as an 'umbrella term' to describe 'the entire complex and multi-step processes used to extract value from data' with real-world implications.

The term 'cultural analytics', coined by Lev Manovich in 2007, refers to exploring and analysing massive cultural data sets of visual material. Here cultural analytics is framed as 'mining data and then visualising data'. Furthermore, Manovich (2016, p. 10) explains that cultural analytics is interested in the 'patterns that can be derived from the analysis of large cultural datasets'. Here we see that the term 'cultural analytics' is very similar to that of data analytics, as a process of discovering insights and patterns from cultural data.

Although similar, the aim of cultural data science is its grounding as a scientific discipline, where one poses questions and applies interdisciplinary methodologies to test hypotheses in extracting values from cultural data. Cultural data science is also embedded in praxis and real-world applications, creating frameworks for generating knowledge and toolkits that policy-makers and market agents use to understand and influence the underpinnings of human culture and society. Indeed, the Centre for Social and Cultural Data Science at McGill University illustrates this focus on 'real-world impact'. Cultural data science differs from cultural analytics in its focus on real-world, practical application. Moreover, cultural data science acknowledges that decision-makers and governance structures for cultural policies and institutions reside in urban areas, and it aims to work closely with them, whereas cultural analytics presently lacks frameworks for influencing policy and instead focuses on 'analysing cultural trends'.

Presently, the concept of cultural data science has yet to be clearly defined, therefore this paper attempts to provide a first definition. Cultural data science is a unification of several academic fields (see Fig. 1) aiming to respect and honour the ideas, methodologies, and tools developed by a set of contiguous disciplines and—to use Irizarry's (2020) definition—adapt these to create an entire complex and multistep process for extracting value from cultural data. Cultural data science can be thought of as an extension of urban studies and cultural studies, collecting data from various sources and applying advanced computational methods to test hypotheses and devise new frameworks for influencing policy and market dynamics. For example, if a city takes a data-driven, evidence-led approach to

Figure 1: A Venn diagram explaining cultural data science

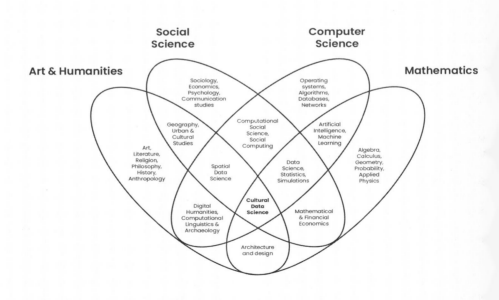

vishalkumar.london ©

nplement a new cultural policy, the methodologies inherent to cultural data sci-
nce can assist and guide the entire procedure, working together with architects, de-
elopers, residents, and cultural institutions. If the task is to understand the dynam-
s of culture, cultural data science can work alongside other disciplines and research
elds, bringing computational techniques to the table.

eferences

ar, V. (2013). "Data science and prediction." *Communications of the ACM* 56.12: pp.64–73.

rverbom, M. and Murray, J. (2018). "Datastructuring—Organizing and curating digital
traces into action." *Big Data & Society* 5.2: p.2053951718799114.

yashi, C. (1998). "What is data science? Fundamental concepts and a heuristic example."
C. Hayashi, K. Yajima, H. Bock, N. Ohsumi, Y. Tanaka, Y. Baba ed. *In Data science, classification, and related methods.* Tokyo.

arry, R.A. (2020). "The role of academia in data science education." *Harvard Data Science
Review* 2.1.

anovich, L. (2016). "The Science of Culture? Social Computing, Digital Humanities and
Cultural Analytics." *Journal of Cultural Analytics* 10.22148/16.004.

anovich, L. (2017). "Cultural data: Possibilities and limitations of the digitized archives."
Museum and archive on the move. Changing cultural institutions in the digital era,
pp.259–276.

eng, X.L. (2019). "Data science: An artificial ecosystem." *Harvard Data Science Review* 1.1.

orris, J.W. (2015). "Curation by code: Infomediaries and the data mining of taste." *European journal of cultural studies* 18.4-5: pp.446–463.

wer, D.J., Heavin, C., McDermott, J. and Daly, M. (2018). "Defining business analytics:
an empirical approach." *Journal of Business Analytics* 1.1: pp. 40–53.

senbaum, S. (2011). *Curation nation: How to win in a world where consumers are
creators.* New York City.

ftwarestudies. Lev Manovich. (n.d.) *The Science of Culture? Social Computing, Digital
Humanities and Cultural Analytics Studying Big Cultural Data: Social Computing and
Digital Humanities,* viewed 24 November 2020 http://manovich.net/content/04-proj-
ects/089-cultural-analytics-social-computing/cultural_analytics_article_final.pdf.

ftwarestudies. Lev Manovich. (n.d.) *Cultural analytics: visualising cultural patterns in the
era of "more media',* viewed 24 November 2020 http://manovich.net/content/
04-projects/064-cultural-analytics-visualizing-cultural-patterns/60_article_2009.pdf.

5. A Deep Image of the City: A Generative Approach to Urban Design Visualisation

Ariel Noyman/Kent Larson

Abstract

Streetscape visualisations are necessary for the understanding and evaluation of urban design alternatives. Alongside blueprints and textual descriptions, these design aids can affect city-form, building-codes, and regulations for decades. However, despite major advances in computer graphics, crafting high-quality streetscape visualisations is still a complex, lengthy, and costly task, especially for real-time multiparty design sessions. Here DeepScope, a generative, lightweight, and real-time platform for urban planning and Cityscapes visualisation is presented. DeepScope is composed of a Deep Convolutional Generative Neural Network (DCGAN) and a Tangible User Interface (TUI) designed for multi-participant urban design sessions and real-time feedback. Implementing DeepScope in urban design processes can expedite design iterations and improve the understanding of design outcomes. Unlike traditional techniques, this tool allows designers to focus on urban programming or massing exercises, without the need for complex visualisation processes or costly rendering setups. This approach could support urban design processes that are enhanced by the visual atmosphere and impressions of *The Image of the City*. This paper explores the design, development, and deployment of the DeepScope platform, as well as discussing the potential implementation of DeepScope in urban design processes.

Introduction: The Imageability of the City

*understand the role of environmental images in our own urban
es (...) we needed to develop and test the idea of imageability (...)
d thus to suggest some principles for urban design. (Lynch 1960)*

rban design renderings and streetscape visualisations are es-
ntial for designers, stakeholders, and decision-makers during
ty-design processes. These visual aids can clarify the outcomes
complex design decisions, such as zoning, building codes, or
nd-use allocations, with the potential to affect urban develop-
ent for decades to come (Smith et al. 1998; Al-Kodmany 1999).
chitects and planners have been aware of the importance of
nderstating the impacts of urban design on the street-level for
nturies, however they often lacked the medium and techniques
communicate these effects (Batty et al. 2000).

Figure 1: *The Image of the City*:
Lynch "imageability" dissects the city
into experiential fragments, in which
the individual fragments are combined
to create the streetscape.

District

Node

Edge

Landmark

Path

his seminal 1960 book, Kevin Lynch introduced "imageability" as
novel approach to the visual perception of urban environments
nch 1960, p. 9). Lynch suggested a toolset for the classification
city-form, in which nodes, landmarks, paths, edges, and districts
flect the sensation of transitioning through the urban scape. In
e *View From the Road* study (Appleyard et al. 1964), the "image-
ility" paradigm was tested using a new medium: Lynch mount-
a dashcam to a car and went on several rides around Boston
d other U.S. cities (Andrews 2007). Later, these recordings were

sped up and played, to reflect the overall "feel" of the road tri
Lynch proposed overlooking the fine-grained street elements
architecture, and instead focused on the "imageability" of the u
ban outline: what is the composition of the built mass? Wh
shapes the street-section? Are there any noticeable landmarks?
the years to come, these documentation techniques of Kev
Lynch became standard tools in the field of urban design (Ca
and Schissler 1969; Pearce and Fagence 1996).

1.1 The Challenge of Visualisation

Despite Lynch's contribution to the visual perception of cities, th
documentation of existing environments is not sufficient for a
curately predicting the impact of future interventions. As Bat
concludes, urban visualisations are critical during the initial d
sign stages—when the context of the design challenge is bei
established—as well as to the generation and evaluation of alte
native designs (Batty et al. 2000). In the last decades, advances
Computer-Aided Design (CAD) and computer graphics introduce
numerous tools for visualising future urban developmen
(Shiode 2000; Kempenaar 2016). Yet, despite their abundance, on
a few offer tools for real-time, urban visualisations during colla
orative design processes (Mueller et al. 2018). Most CAD tools r
quire complex setups, costly hard- and software, while deman
ing steep learning curves (Yan 2014; Mekni and Lemieux 201
Further, these tools often require users to set up many control p
rameters in virtual environments, such as cameras, lights, mate
als, or shaders. This process quickly becomes laborious in comple
design scenes, and can gravely affect the outcome, cost, and dur
tion of visualisation processes (Lovett et al. 2015).

Moreover, standard CAD user interfaces rarely suppo
multi-user collaborative design, greatly limiting the active partic
pation of stakeholders in iterative design sessions, and forcing a
asynchronous decision-making process. This means early urba
design stages suffer from a lack of design details so hindering r
alistic visualisations. These stages commonly involve crude mas
ing exercises and lack street-level details, such that visualisatio
are schematic at best (Drettakis et al. 2007; Brusaporci 2017).

Figure 2: DeepScope TUI: Multiple users can simultaneously interact and discuss urban design iterations. The table-top is used both as the design space and as a schematic urban top-view. The vertical monitor visualises the DCGAN street view.

DeepScope: Methodology and System Design

This paper presents DeepScope, a collaborative, tangible, and real-time urban design and visualisation platform. DeepScope allows multiple users to perform early urban design and land-use allocation sessions collaboratively, observing the outcomes as realistic streetscape visuals. Unlike CAD tools, DeepScope offers minimal setup, along with simple and cheap hard- and software, while requiring no expertise to use.

Figure 3: Top row: Model trained on Cityscapes dataset, deployed as node.js app.

Bottom row: TUI triggers DCGAN renderings.

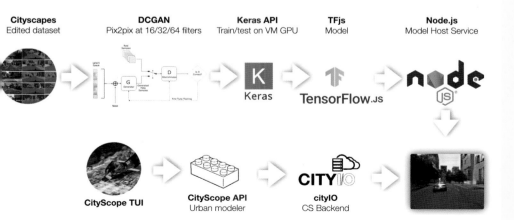

Cityscapes	DCGAN	Keras API	TFjs	Node.js
Edited dataset	Pix2pix at 16/32/64 filters	Train/test on VM GPU	Model	Model Host Service

CityScope TUI	CityScope API	cityIO	
	Urban modeler	CS Backend	

This section details the main parts of DeepScope as: a Tangible User Interface (TUI) for rapid urban prototyping; and Deep Conditional Generative Adversarial Network (DCGAN) for visualisation. As users interact with the TUI, a virtual city model is procedurally updated and fed into the DCGAN model. The models then generate a Cityscapes visualisation based on the user-selected view. The rest of this section explores the components of DeepScope, TUI and the dataset, model training and results.

2.1 HCI Platform for Rapid Urban Prototyping

DeepScope Tangible User Interface (TUI) is built for iterative urban design and land-use allocation. This TUI offers a playful, multi-user design environment which is tangible and augmented by real-time visualisation.

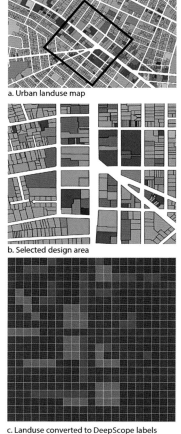

Figure 4: DeepScope process: (a,b) designating an urban intervention site (c, d) translating land-use/zoning bounds and user-interaction into (e) procedural 3-D environment and passing it to DCGAN model for (f) generation of a street-view visualisation

a. Urban landuse map

b. Selected design area

c. Landuse converted to DeepScope labels

d. DeepScope TUI and "Observer"

e. Observer captures are input for the DCGAN

f. DCGAN Streetview perspective output

raditional Computer-Aided Design (CAD) tools were commonly uilt around a single user with limited inputs (mouse and key-oard) and outputs (monitor and printer). Initially, these interfac-s were not conceived as collaborative design tools, even when omputer networks became mainstream (Sutherland 1964; Batty t al. 2000).

the past decades, the development of several TUIs facilitated ollaborative urban design, augmented by computational analyt-s. Among these are the Augmented Urban Planning Workbench, ne I/O Bulb, The Clay Table, and Sensetable (Ishii et al. 2002; Ishii t al. 2004; Patten et al. 2001)—all built to enable teamwork and ollaboration. The MIT *City Science group* is developing CityScope CS): an urban modelling, simulation, and collaborative deci-on-making platform. CS merges TUIs and analytical modules to upport a collaborative, evidence-based discourse around the uilt environment (Noyman 2015). For this research, a CS instance as developed, constructed, and tested in an active demonstra-on space at the MIT Media Lab in Cambridge, Massachusetts.

Figure 5: Multi-user interaction with DeepScope. Depending on the scale and extent of the urban context, design sessions can accommodate up to fifteen users.

2.2 DeepScope User Interaction

The TUI consists of three components: a physical urban model, a scanning module, and a feedback module. The urban model includes an arbitrary grid of 4x4 LEGO tiles, tagged with binary patterns. Each pattern is a 16-bit code of black or white 1x1 LEGO studs, allowing over 65,000 unique pre-defined land-uses and attributes. Each grid-cell pattern, represents a different streetscape class: roads, buildings, green-spaces, parking, sidewalks, etc. Each class contains additional parameters, such as height, volume, shape, rotation, or density. Table 1 specifies the classes and their attributes. When users shift a tile, the scanning module detects the interaction through a scanning and networking tool using OpenCV and Node.js. Lastly, a feedback module, containing monitors and projectors, communicates the interaction and analysis outcomes back to the users. This interface enables rapid design iteration, facilitates collaboration, and engages users in urban design processes (Noyman 2015; Noyman et al. 2017).

Table 1: Cityscapes classes: Marked with plus (+) are labels which can be altered dynamically using CS TUI. Marked with star (*) are labels that are generated dynamically in the 3-D model.

Group	Summary
flat	road*+; sidewalk*+ parking*+; rail track
human	person*; riders*
vehicle	car*; truck*; bus*; on rails; motorcycle; bicycle; caravan; trailer
construction	building; wall*; fence; guard rail; bridge
object	pole*; pole group; traffic sign*; traffic light*
nature	vegetation*+; terrain
sky	sky*
void	ground; dynamic; static

2.3 Procedural Cityscapes Environment

With each interaction, the scanner decodes the new grid-cell patterns, updating the table's data structure. This triggers a regeneration of a virtual 3-D environment, in which each grid-cell is represented by class and additional parameters. As users allocate tiles, the environment is filled with streetscape elements: a vegetation pattern creates a surface with procedural trees, bushes, or live-fences; a sidewalk pattern produces pedestrian and street-signage; while a parking-lot pattern will proliferate with parked vehicles. This 3-D environment is uniformly hued with RGB values that correspond to input classes, anticipated by the Neural Network model. The scanning and 3-D scene generation are carried out on the client-side web-browser using a simple webcam and a WebGL program (Mrdoob 2019).

4 Observer

The urban environment designed by the users is continuously "photographed" by the "observer" grid-cell. Similar to Lynch's *The View from the Road* (Appleyard, et al. 1964), this unique pattern mimics a virtual nomad in the city, allowing users to set its position, point-of-view and angle. The observer baseline parameters (such as Field of View, Frustum, and height) approximate the camera calibration appendix of the Cityscapes dataset (Cordts et al. 2016). Additional camera controls were implemented to allow users to move, rotate, pan, or zoom the "observer" by relocating the cell itself via a custom game-pad joystick (see figure 7).

5 Table-Top Augmentation

The TUI table-top, therefore becomes the design space as well as the visualisation canvas. With each design iteration, an illuminated land-use diagram is projected onto the table-top so that each tile is showing its respective pattern, name, or parameter (density, land use, etc). The observer position is displayed using a perspective cone that indicates its viewing angle and FOV. Together, Deep-Scope TUI components allow multiple users to design and amend the urban environment and observe the effects of different scenarios on its streetscape.

Figure 6: TUI interactions are analysed using OpenCV and streamed as JSON with the webGL app. A 3-D model is created based on the JSON array and the observer viewing angle. Lastly, a snapshot image feeds an input vector to the DCGAN model. TUI: (1) Observer position (2) Observer view angle and FOV cone (3) Observer's 3-D street-view as input for DCGAN (4) DCGAN model prediction of street-view (5) TUI interactive grid.

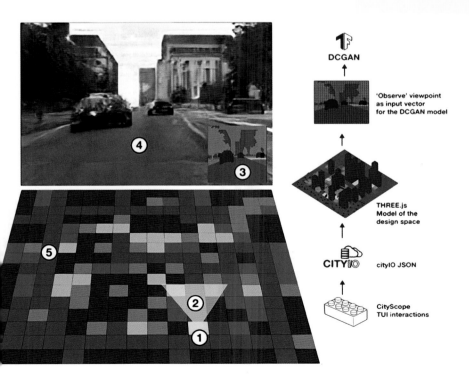

DCGAN

'Observe' viewpoint as input vector for the DCGAN model

THREE.js Model of the design space

CITYIO   cityIO JSON

CityScope TUI interactions

3 DeepScope Generative Neural Network

In order to produce realistic street-view visualisation, DeepScope implement a Neural Network (NN) variant called Deep Convolutional Generative Adversarial Network (DCGAN). Following TUI interactions, the observer's viewpoint is captured and converted into an input vector for the DCGAN NN. The DCGAN NN predicts an image corresponding to the input vector, where each pixel in the input vector triggers a pixel in the DCGAN output. The resulting image draws onto the DeepScope feedback module. This section explores the data set, model architecture, and NN training.

3.1 Dataset and Model Training

Accurate pattern recognition using NN has been feasible since the late 1980s (LeCun et al. 1989). However, generating new data that concatenate a given dataset well is still considered a complex problem within the scope of machine learning (Creswell 2018). Data generation using NN greatly advanced with the introduction of Generative Adversarial Networks (GANs) (Goodfellow et al. 2013). GANs use two competing NNs, the "generator" and "discriminator" that "adverse" each other. The generator attempts to create new data (such as image, sound, or text) and the discriminator aims to nullify these "fake" creations. The training is complete when the generator creates indistinguishable samples that continually fail the discriminator (Isola et al. 2017).

3.2 Image-to-Image Translation

Conditional GAN (CGAN) is a branch of GAN in which both the NN are given additional data to focus the generation on specific targets (Mirza and Osindero 2014; Salimans et al. 2016). A special use-case of CGAN is a pixel-wise conditional generation of images, also known as Image to Image Translation (I2I), or pix2pix (Isola et al. 2017; Isola et al. 2016). In I2I, the pixel values of one image are used as labels of the other, while image pairs are used for training. This allows pixel-level prediction using a spatial classification of regions in the image (Arjovsky, et al. 2017). In practice, CGANs extends a classic GAN loss function:

$$\min_{G} \max_{D} V(D,G) = E_{x \sim P_{data}(x)} \left[\log D\left(x|y\right) \right] + E_{z \sim p_{z}(z)} \left[\log\left(1 - D\left(G(z|y)\right)\right) \right]$$

Here, function V of Generator and Discriminator G, D attempts to minimize a delta between ground-truth data x (in this case, the pixel data) and z, which is the accumulated pixel distribution learnt on each training step. Unlike classic GANs, log $D(x \mid y)$ denotes that the additional "class" data y conditions the learning on both data x as well as on y class. In this respect, distributions created by cGAN generator do not only share resemblance to the learning dataset, but are trained to mimic high-level data structure.

Figure 7: (left) User interaction with grid-cells. (right) "Observer" viewing angle, depth and position is set via an Arduino Gamepad.

Figure 8: Test samples of different epochs during training: right column shows quality degradation beyond 200 epochs.

3 Cityscapes Dataset

DeepScope's DCGAN model trains on the Cityscapes dataset (Cordts et al. 2016). Cityscapes are composed of pairs of street-view images that were taken around 50 European cities using a dashcam—during different seasons, times of day, and weather conditions. Each pair includes a street-view image and a corresponding segmented image with 30 semantic labels. These labels represent different streetscape classes, from buildings and roads to licence-plates and road signs. For DeepScope, a pre-processing algorithm was designed to remove motion-blur, increase sharpness, saturation, and remove colour-casting—all of which were common in this dataset.

4 Model Architecture and Performance

The design of DeepScope NN architecture allows fast predictions, minimal setup, and high portability. The generator has 16 layers with a U-Net (Ronneberger, et al. 2015) encoder-decoder structure. For performance purposes, the discriminator has five layers and is using Leaky ReLU activation, shown to improve stability in training (Radford et al. 2015). Commonly, DCGAN models benefit from a high number of filters set to detect patterns on input data (Ronneberger et al. 2015). However, added filters increase the model size, which can gravely impact real-time performance and usability in low-tier devices. In order to maintain attention to fine details, a shallow NN design with a random up-sampling of 150% was designed (Isola et al. 2017). This network design allows deployment on most client-side browsers or even in mobile environments, as long as Node.js and TensorFlow.js are supported (Smilkov et al. 2019).

3.5 DCGAN Training and Results

As previously described in "Model Architecture and Performance portability and speed were crucial factors in balancing in age-quality and model size. Twenty training sessions were performed with 16, 32, 64, and 128 filters, within 50–2000 epochs. Resulting models were converted to a web format and tested for stability and response time on various client devices. A trained model with 64 filters and 200 epochs showed the best overall results. Models with fewer filters produced low-quality result whereas models with 300–2000 epochs demonstrated inconsistencies and "mode collapse" (Arjovsky et al. 2017). Models with more filters were too slow to load and predict in real-time.

3.6 User Interaction Performance Test

Interaction latency was avoided by using two asynchronous processes; first prediction process and then TUI interaction respons In preliminary user tests, the DCGAN model predicts at ~0.66 se prediction, and the TUI showed a fixed response interval of 50m Although the DCGAN slightly trails the TUI, the observatio showed that users tend to focus attention on the TUI before expecting the DCGAN output. In that sense, the overall user-experience could be considered in real-time with continuous desig and-feedback loops (Deber et al. 2015).

4 Discussion and Conclusion

This paper describes DeepScope, a tangible urban design platfor for real-time street-view visualisation. Visualisations are create using a Deep Conditional Generative Adversarial Network (D GAN) trained on the Cityscapes dataset. A Tangible User Interfa for rapid urban prototyping was created for iterations and fee back. The rest of this section discusses the strengths, weakness threats, and opportunities of this work.

4.1 Strengths

The design of DeepScope allows experts and non-professiona alike to collaboratively experiment with urban design scenari and real-time feedback. The platform can augment early stages Cityscapes design with vivid street-view visuals. These stag have significant impacts on the urban form and spatial organis tion of cities, but commonly lack sufficient design representatic (Batty et al. 2000). Unlike traditional CAD tools, DeepScope's pr trained NN carries out the complexity of creating a 3-D urba

ene. Designed for the web, DeepScope is platform agnostic and requires minimal
mputational resources, making it more accessible and portable for public partici-
ation. Lastly, the unpolished nature of the GAN outcome allows designers and reg-
ators to focus on the overall Image of the City instead of undecided details (Lynch
60).

2 Weaknesses

espite the promise of generative NN, GANs continue to have several drawbacks.
rst, GANs require large and properly labelled datasets; as such, creating a new
tyscapes dataset for other geographies which will require significant effort. Sever-
 emerging methods suggest decoupling (Zhu et al. 2017) and label-less learning
ucic 2019), which can simplify the labelling effort. Nevertheless, dataset collection
nd partial labelling would still be required. Moreover, GANs tend to be inconsistent
uring the learning process, as explored in DCGAN Training and Results (Shin 2017).
stly, the DeepScope GAN would not be able to visualise non-street view angles.
nce the Cityscapes dataset was captured using a vehicle dashcam, only matching
ngles will produce reasonable predictions (Salimans et al. 2016). This issue is com-
on amongst supervised NN, and requires either non-supervised methods or more
tensive datasets.

3 Threats

ne rising popularity of GANs is greatly attributed to their ability to "create". Never-
eless, GANs tend to be unpredictable in their results. Within urban design practic-
, a certain degree of "creative freedom" continues to be desired, yet unpredicted
ols might cause resentment or misleading impressions. In DeepScope, the same
reet-view angle with the same urban-design setup might produce different visual
sults if run twice. Whereas the authors perceive this as a design feature and man-
estation of Kevin Lynch's "imageability" concept (Lynch 1960), others might ob-
rve it as a symbol of untamed technology. Additionally, NN is strictly bound by its
chitecture and training data. Tempered NN or datasets can significantly affect the
utcomes of the model and inject bias into the results. With machine-learning tools
ecoming mainstream in the design industry, these concerns should be addressed
 testing, validating, and open-sourcing design tools, models, and data.

4 Opportunities

ne improvement of DeepScope has several aspects: first, emerging NN architec-
ures and training parameters can improve the DCGAN results. Other methods,
ach as Variational Autoencounder or auto GANs, can produce more refined results
ith greater control (Mescheder et al. 2017). Also, extending the training datasets to
fferent urban environments could yield more versatile representations. Lastly, the
JI can be improved to include multi-scale environments and finer-grained editing
pabilities.

4.5 Implementation in Real-World Design Processes

DeepScope is now being tested as part of an extensive urban modelling system built for an international urban design competition in a major European city. The report on this platform and user study will be shared in late 2020. More broadly DeepScope might hint to the future of insightful CAD tools, spanning beyond digital rulers, and drafting aids. Such tools would not only expedite tedious tasks but might offer leverage to the power of advanced computation, towards becoming insightful "design companions".

References

Al-Kodmany, K. (1999). "Using Visualization Techniques for Enhancing Public Participation in Planning and Design: Process, Implementation, and Evaluation." *Landscape and Urban Planning* 45.1: pp. 37–45.

Andrews, M. (2007). "The view from the road and the picturesque." *The Aesthetics of Human Environments* pp. 272–89.

Appleyard, D., K. Lynch, and J. R Myer (1964). *The View from the Road*. MA.

Arjovsky, M., S. Chintala, and L. Bottou (2017) "Wasserstein Generative Adversarial Networks." *International Conference on Machine Learning* 21: pp. 214–23.

Batty, M., D. Chapman, S. Evans, M. Haklay, S. Kueppers, N. Shiode, A. Smith, and P. M Torrens (2000). *Visualizing the City: Communicating Urban Design to Planners and Decision-Makers*.

Brusaporci, S. (2017). "The Importance of Being Honest: Issues of Transparency in Digital Visualization of Architectural Heritage." *3D Printing: Breakthroughs in Research and Practice* 333.60 IGI Global.

Carr, S., and D. Schissler (1969). "The City as a Trip: Perceptual Selection and Memory in the View from the Road." *Environment and Behavior* 1.1: p. 7.

Cordts, M., M. Omran, S. Ramos, T. Rehfeld, M. Enzweiler, R. Benenson, U. Franke, S. Roth, and B. Schiele (2016). *The Cityscapes Dataset for Semantic Urban Scene Understanding* viewed 02 April 2021, http://arxiv.org/abs/1604.01685.

Creswell, A., T. White, V. Dumoulin, K. Arulkumaran, B. Sengupta, and A. A Bharath (2018). IEEE *Signal Processing Magazine* 35.1: pp 53–65.

Deber, J., R. Jota, C. Forlines, and D. Wigdor (2015). "How Much Faster Is Fast Enough?: User Perception of Latency & Latency Improvements in Direct and Indirect Touch." Proceedings of the 33rd Annual Acm *Conference on Human Factors in Computing System* 1827–36. ACM.

Drettakis, G., M. Roussou, A. Reche, and N. Tsingos (2007). "Design and Evaluation of a Real-World Virtual Environment for Architecture and Urban Planning." Presence: *Teleoperators and Virtual Environments* 16.3.: pp. 318–32.

odfellow, I., J. Pouget-Abadie, M. Mirza, B. Xu, D. Warde-Farley, S. Ozair, A. Courville, and Y. Bengio (2013). "Front Matter." *Environmental Fluid Dynamics*, viewed 02 April 2021, https://doi.org/10.1016/B978-0-12-088571-8.01001-9.

ii, H., E. Ben-Joseph, J. Underkoffler, L. Yeung, D. Chak, Z. Kanji, and B. Piper (2002). "Augmented Urban Planning Workbench: Overlaying Drawings, Physical Models and Digital Simulation." *Proceedings of the 1st International Symposium on Mixed and Augmented Reality*, 203. IEEE Computer Society.

ii, H., C. Ratti, B. Piper, Y. Wang, A. Biderman, and E. Ben-Joseph (2004). "Bringing Clay and Sand into Digital Design—Continuous Tangible User Interfaces." *BT Technology Journal* 22.4: pp. 287–99.

la, P., J. Zhu, T. Zhou, and A. A .Efros (2016). "Image-to-Image Translation with Conditional Adversarial Networks." *Arxiv*.

la P., J. Zhu, Z. Tinghui, A.A. Efros (2017). "Image-to-Image Translation with Conditional Adversarial Networks." In *Proceedings of the Ieee Conference on Computer Vision and Pattern Recognition*, pp. 1125–34.

mpenaar, Annet, J. Westerink, M. van Lierop, M. Brinkhuijsen, and A. van den Brink (2016). "Design Makes You Understand"—Mapping the Contributions of Designing to Regional Planning and Development." *Landscape and Urban Planning* 149: pp. 20–30.

Cun, Y., B. Boser, J. S. Denker, D. Henderson, R. E Howard, W. Hubbard, and L. D. Jackel (1989). "Backpropagation Applied to Handwritten Zip Code Recognition." *Neural Computation* 1.4: pp. 541–51.

rett, A., K. Appleton, B. Warren-Kretzschmar, and C. Von Haaren (2015). "Using 3D Visualization Methods in Landscape Planning: An Evaluation of Options and Practical Issues." *Landscape and Urban Planning* 148: pp. 85–94.

tic, M., M. Tschannen, M. Ritter, X. Zhai, O. Bachem, and S. Gelly (2019). "High-Fidelity Image Generation with Fewer Labels." *arXiv Preprint arXiv:1903.02271*.

ach, K. (1960). *The Image of the City*. Vol. 11. Cambridge, MA..

kni, M., and A. Lemieux (2014). "Augmented Reality: Applications, Challenges and Future Trends." *Applied Computational Science* 205.14.

scheder, L., S. Nowozin, and A. Geiger (2017). "Adversarial Variational Bayes: Unifying Variational Autoencoders and Generative Adversarial Networks." In *Proceedings of the 34th International Conference on Machine Learning*. JMLR. org. 70, 2391–2400.

rza, M., and S. Osindero (2014). "Conditional Generative Adversarial Nets." *arXiv Preprint arXiv:1411.1784*.

doob (2019). "Mrdoob/Three.js." *GitHub*, viewed 02 April 2021, https://github.com/mrdoob/three.js.

eller, J., H. Lu, A. Chirkin, B. Klein, and G. Schmitt (2018). "Citizen Design Science: A Strategy for Crowd-Creative Urban Design." *Cities* 72: 181–88.

yman, A. (2015). "POWERSTRUCTURES: The Urban Form of Regulation." (Master's thesis) *Massachusetts Institute of Technology*, viewed 02 April 2021, https://dspace.mit.edu/handle/1721.1/99301.

yman, A., T. Holtz, J. Kröger, J. R. Noennig, and K. Larson (2017) "Finding Places: HCI Platform for Public Participation in Refugees' Accommodation Process." *Procedia Computer Science*, viewed 02 April 2021, https://doi.org/10.1016/j.procs.2017.08.180.

ten, J., H. Ishii, J. Hines, and G. Pangar (2001). "Sensetable: A Wireless Object Tracking Platform for Tangible User Interfaces." *Proceedings of the Sigchi Conference on Human Factors in Computing Systems* 253.60. ACM.

arce, P. L., and M. Fagence (1996). "The Legacy of Kevin Lynch: Research Implications." *Annals of Tourism Research* 23.3: pp. 576–98.

Radford, A., L. Metz, and S. Chintala (2015). *Unsupervised Representation Learning with Deep Convolutional Generative Adversarial Networks*, viewed 03. April 2021, http:/ arxiv.org/abs/1511.06434.

Ronneberger, O., P. Fischer, and T. Brox (2015). "U-Net: Convolutional Networks for Biomedical Image Segmentation." *International Conference on Medical Image Computing and Computer-Assisted Intervention*, Intervention 234. 41.

Salimans, T., I. Goodfellow, W. Zaremba, V. Cheung, A. Radford, and X. Chen (2016). "Improved Techniques for Training Gans." *Advances in Neural Information Processing Systems* 2234. 42.

Shin, H., J. Kwon Lee, J. Kim, and J. Kim (2017). "Continual Learning with Deep Generative Replay." *Advances in Neural Information Processing Systems* 2990-9.

Shiode, N. (2000). "3D Urban Models: Recent Developments in the Digital Modelling Urban Environments in Three-Dimensions." *GeoJournal* 52.3: pp. 263–69.

Smilkov, D., N. Thorat, Y. Assogba, A. Yuan, N. Kreeger, P. Yu, and K. Zhang (2019). "TensorFlow. Js: Machine Learning for the Web and Beyond." *arXiv* Preprint arXiv:1901.05350.

Smith, A., M. Dodge, and S. Doyle (1998). "Visual Communication in Urban Planning and Urban Design." *University College London, Centre for Advanced Spatial Analys (CASA).*

Sutherland, I.E. (1964). "Sketchpad a Man-Machine Graphical Communication System *Simulation* 2.5: pp. R–3.

Yan, J. (2014). "An Evaluation of Current Applications of 3D Visualization Software in Landscape Architecture." (Master's thesis) Utah State University.

Zhu, J., T. Park, P. Isola, and A.A. Efros (2017). "Unpaired Image-to-Image Translation Using Cycle-Consistent Adversarial Networks." *Proceedings of the Ieee International Conference on Computer Vision* 2223.32.

6. Monitoring Health-Related Features of Urban Neighbourhoods with Differing Social Status

Evgenia Yosifova/Jörg Pohlan

Abstract

Social status and the urban living environment are among the key determinants of human health. In Germany, there are several examples of social monitoring systems introduced at the small urban scale[1]. Yet, the development of consistent tools for the observation of health-related neighbourhood features lags behind. In this paper, we propose possible approaches to set up a citywide monitoring of health-promoting and damaging characteristics of the living environment taking the city of Hamburg as a case study. First, we outline neighbourhood features with a scientifically proven influence on health and suggest indicators to measure them. Air and noise pollution, heat load, public green spaces, walkability, healthcare infrastructure and access to food, alcohol and tobacco are topics discussed in further detail. We focus on the necessary data, its availability and the consistency in the methodology used for its generation. Next, we provide a brief overview of

1 In this paper, the terms "small urban scale" and "neighbourhood scale" are used interchangeably.

current limitations concerning the regular update of the monito
ing. We conclude with an outlook on the necessity and the poter
tial gain from the suggested instrument, especially in light of th
COVID-19 pandemic. Finally, we point out the most essential step
for introducing the proposed monitoring of health-related neigh
bourhood features.

1. Social Status, Urban Neighbourhoods and their Health-Relate Features

Several studies indicate that social status has an important im
pact on human health. High social status generally means highe
income and better education. Thus, it implies easier access t
quality healthcare and a healthier lifestyle, since the highe
awareness of potential health risks fosters regular physical exe
cise and the maintaining of a healthy diet (Moscelli et al. 2018,
303; Pampel et al. 2010, p. 356–358). Additionally, social status d
termines where in the city residents can afford to live, i.e., wha
access they have to health-promoting resources and to what e:
tent are they exposed to health-damaging environmental inflµ
ences: "The rich live where they want to, the poor live where the
ought to" (Häußermann 2008, p. 336).

   Health-promoting and damaging features of the urban env
ronment tend to be unevenly distributed within the spati
realms of larger cities. More often than not, there is a concentra
tion of unfavourable environmental influences in socially d
prived areas (Böhme and Köckler 2018, p. 88). Furthermore, a
cess to health-promoting resources such as public green space
or playgrounds in these neighbourhoods is usually less conve
nient compared to more affluent urban areas (Ferguson et a
2018, p. 143). In this context, the concept of environmental justic
deserves special attention. It aims to counteract the uneven bu
den carried by specific population groups in their exposure to
multitude of health-damaging environmental influences, e.g
heat island effects, noise pollution and poor air quality (Europe
an Environment Agency [EEA] 2019, p. 1). This burden dispropo
tionally affects population groups of lower socio-econom
standing—who are left with no choice but to live in neighbou
hoods with lower rents, more likely to be situated in the vicini
of industrial areas or busy arterial roads.

In cities such as Berlin and Hamburg, for example, so-called "s
cial monitoring systems" were introduced in order to continu
ously observe social deprivation patterns at the small scale (Se

sverwaltung für Stadtentwicklung und Wohnen 2019; Behörde
r Stadtentwicklung und Wohnen [BSW] 2019). This contributes
a more efficient distribution of the limited financial resources
public authorities for the implementation of urban regenera-
n measures. However, in the spatial context of German cities,
r less attention is given to the consistent monitoring of
alth-related neighbourhood features, such as measuring dis-
butions of available urban resources and threats. To date, only
rlin has introduced a so-called *Umweltatlas* (*environmental
las*). The use of geodata allowed the spatial overlaying of dif-
rent environmental factors with a direct impact on health:
ise, air pollutants (PM2,5 and NO2), accessibility of green spac-
and heat load (Klimeczek 2011).

In this regard, the following questions arise: To what extent
n a similar approach be applied in other cities? What are the
erequisites to monitor health-promoting and damaging fea-
res of the urban living environment at the small urban scale?

Monitoring Health-Related Features of Hamburg's Neighbour-
ods

this paper, we use data sources and spatial structures of the city
Hamburg to find out if and how health-promoting and damag-
g characteristics of neighbourhoods can be continuously moni-
red. To that end, we focus on: setting up indicators, data selec-
n and current limitations.

Indicators and Data Selection

fining valid and robust indicators is the first step towards al-
ving a citywide comparison of urban neighbourhoods in terms
their health-related features. In the course of the research proj-
t "Healthy Neighbourhoods"[2] (2017–2021), we developed a list of
dicators in order to assess the possible impacts of specific
ighbourhood characteristics on human health. The experience
gained in terms of obtaining the necessary data allowed us to
ngle out the indicators, which can be used for a citywide moni-
ring of the health-promoting and damaging features of urban
ighbourhoods. For instance, establishing a comprehensive qual-
assessment of every public green space in Hamburg is not fea-
ble while implementing annual or biannual data collection sys-
ms, depending on the interval chosen for monitoring updates.
ternatively, estimating the proportion of residents with access
public green spaces within a walking distance of 500 metres is

2 "Gesundheitsförderung und
Prävention im Setting Quartier"
(short: "Gesunde Quartiere");
http://www.gesundequartiere.de/

a plausible indicator for comparing urban neighbourhoods terms of public green space accessibility.

Against this background, the next paragraphs are dedicate to proposing indicators suitable for a citywide small-scale heal monitoring for the city of Hamburg. These indicators are d signed to measure health-related features of the urban enviro ment only and do not take into account the individual heal situation at the neighbourhood level. We recommend setting monitoring at the level of the so-called "statistical areas"[3] Hamburg in order to ensure its compatibility with the alrea existing Social Monitoring (BSW 2019). Thus, the cumulative bu den of social deprivation and possible adverse effects of the ban environment on human health can be easily identified wit in the spatial structure of the city.

Data selection will be discussed for each of the proposed i dicators. We focus mainly on the use of available geodata as resource which can play an important role in monitorir health-related features of the urban environment. For instan geodata allows calculation of the extent of exposure health-damaging levels of outdoor noise. Besides considering p tential hazards posed by the environment, geodata enables taki stock of available health resources as well. The accessibility public green spaces, playgrounds and sports facilities as well the diversity of food supply can be estimated and compared at t neighbourhood level. Moreover, a cartographic visualisation health-promoting and damaging neighbourhood characteristi would allow the identification of areas in need of intervention.

For a comprehensive, and at the same time not overly compl overview, we propose indicators aimed at addressing sever health-related features of the urban environment discussed in number of scientific studies. These include heat load, air and noi pollution, public green spaces, walkability, healthcare and acce to food, alcohol and tobacco. The corresponding indicators a summarised in Table 1 and further discussed in the followir paragraphs. More detailed information about the methodolo of indicator computations and the corresponding data sourc can be found in the book summarising the results of the resear project "Healthy Neighbourhoods" (Yosifova and Pohlan 2021).

3 There are a total of 941 statistical areas with an average population of 2.000 people.

4 Proportion of population living in the given statistical area (applies to all proposed indicators)

5 70-80%: historic district, perimeter development from the 1920s and the 1930s; 80–90%: perimeter development from the Gründerzeit, industrial area, commercial area, administration and office buildings; 90–100%: roads, ports, train stations, depots, etc. (BUE 2020)

Table 1. Indicators for monitoring health-promoting and damaging features of urban neighbourhoods

Features	Indicators
Heat load	Proportion of the population[4] living in an area with a soil sealing degree of more than 70%.
Air pollution	Proportion of the population living within 50 metres of an arterial road
Noise pollution	Proportion of the population exposed to health-damaging noise levels from road, rail, or air traffic
	Proportion of the population living more than 500 metres from the nearest public green space (> 0,5 ha)
Green spaces	Proportion of the population living more than 500 metres from the nearest public green space (> 0,5 ha)
Walkability	Walkability index
Healthcare	Proportion of the population living more than 500 metres from the nearest pharmacy
	Number of residents per pharmacy within 500 metres
	Number of residents per family practice and dental practice within 500 metres
Access to food, alcohol and tobacco	Proportion of the population living more than 500 metres from the nearest fruit and vegetable store
	Proportion of the population living within 500 metres of the nearest fast-food restaurant
	Proportion of the population living within 500 metres of the nearest alcohol and tobacco outlet

1.1. Heat Load

Soil sealing is one of the main factors contributing to heat stress (Hetz et al. 2018, p. 1). When the degree of soil sealing exceeds 70%, which is common in perimeter block buildings dating from the 1920s and the 1930s, excessive heat load with adverse public health effects is highly likely (Behörde für Umwelt und Energie — Local Public Authority for Environment and Energy [BUE] 2017a; BUE 2017b).

In order to determine the extent of the population affected, geodata about soil sealing can be downloaded from Hamburg's Master Portal. This data is derived from a biotope mapping carried out every five years by the *Behörde für Umwelt und Energie*. The biotope types, such as bodies of water, farmland, forests, single-family house developments, perimeter developments, etc. are assigned to ten soil sealing classes, each in a 10-per cent-level (BUE 2020). So far, the data has been updated in a five-year-interval and the estimation methodology has remained consistent. Therefore, we consider the available data reliable enough for estimating the proposed indicator:

Proportion of population living in an area with a soil sealing degree of over 70%[5].

The other necessary data source is the aggregate population at the address or building level. This data can be obtained from Hamburg's Einwohner-Zentralamt (Central Registration Office). The proposed indicator will allow filtering of neighbourhoods based on their share of inhabitants potentially exposed to harmful levels of heat load. This selection can serve as one of the spatial overlays in the mapping of multiple health burdens.

1.2. Air Pollution

Air pollution carries a number of health risks. However, a citywide small-scale monitoring of different air pollutants is currently not an option in Hamburg because of the small number of official measuring stations. As an alternative, we propose esti mating the

Proportion of population living within 50 metres of an arterial road

at the neighbourhood level. The sheer volume of traffic on arterial roads implies high concentration of air pollutants, leaving nearby building residents at a greate risk of adverse health effects such as respiratory illness and reduced lung functio (Sanderson et al. 2005, p. 93).

In general, the highest concentrations of air pollutants are found within th first 50–100 metres of roads and their extent varies depending on the configura tion of the buildings, local topography, weather conditions, and type of pollu ants (Sanderson et al. 2005, p. 94). In order to provide a measure which will no deliver exaggerated exposure results, we propose taking the shortest distance o 50 metres between the buildings and the arterial roads for computation of th indicator.

Estimation of the proposed indicator at the neighbourhood level requires the co ordinates of the arterial roads and residential buildings as geodata, and the aggre gate population numbers at the address or building level. In the case of Hambur this data is publicly available (Master Portal; Central Registration Office), therefor including the indicator in a citywide health monitoring is theoretically unproblem atic. Still, the indicator has one deficiency — the position of the arterial roads withi the city's structure is constant. Therefore, any changes over time will only be ac counted for by alterations in the resident population, in the case of building densif cation, which often includes new residential construction along main urban roads

2.1.3. Noise Pollution

According to a number of studies, noise pollution is one of the main health-damag ing features of the urban environment (Goines and Hagler 2007, pp. 289–291). I this regard, we propose two indicators to carry out a small-scale assessment o long-term exposure to excess noise:

Proportion of population exposed to health-damaging noise levels
from road, rail, or air traffic
Proportion of population exposed to health-damaging noise levels
from multiple sources

Empirical evidence indicates that volume levels of 55 dB(A) at night (Lnight) an 65 dB(A) on average (Lden) carry the risk of harmful effects on human healt (Arndt 2012, p. 91; Schwedler 2008, p. 1). Therefore, these indicators will allow iden tifying areas in need of intervention. For this, two data sources are needed — th aggregate number of neighbourhood inhabitants (either at the building or ad dress level) and, ideally, geodata regarding noise pollution.

The Master Portal of the city of Hamburg provides access to geodata abou noise pollution from road, rail and air traffic as well as heavy industry. Neverthe less, there are some limitations of the available data to be considered. First of a

e data is based on estimates related to traffic volume rather than actual mea-
urements of noise levels. For road traffic, this means that the noise is estimated
r those streets where traffic volume data is available. As a result, a proportion of
ie total noise pollution, albeit relatively minimal, is omitted. Second, the avail-
ble geodata illustrates the dispersal of outdoor noise, thus providing only minor
sight into the actual noise levels affecting residents indoors. Last, but not least,
e estimate of average noise pollution from air traffic fails to depict the highest
oise peaks related to the landing and departure of aeroplanes—which represent
e main annoyance factor. These characteristics and limitations of the available
ata must be taken into account when interpreting the local situation in terms of
oise pollution.

4. Public Green Spaces

cal public green spaces are a valuable health-promoting resource. If well main-
ined and easily accessible, they encourage everyday physical activity, facilitate
ress relief, and provide a physical space for social interaction. Therefore, they (can)
ave favourable physical as well as psychological health effects (Braubach et al. 2017,
189). In the course of the research project "Healthy Neighbourhoods", we devel-
ed methodology for collecting data to measure the quality of green spaces, and
mpare results between several neighbourhoods. As already noted, it is not feasi-
e to carry out and consistently update such an extensive data analysis for the en-
e city of Hamburg. However, the accessibility of green spaces may be assessed by
ing available geodata. This prompts a clear definition of the size of the green
aces and their maximum catchment area. The size is of importance because it
dicates the capacity for outdoor facilities, such as playground equipment, fitness
cilities, benches, rubbish bins, lighting, etc.—the larger the green area, the greater
e variety in the equipment. When assessing the local supply of public green spac-
 in Germany, only those with a minimum size of 0.5 hectare (ha) are considered
öhm et al. 2015, p. 28f.).

Defining the catchment area forms the basis of the accessibility analysis. In
e case of Hamburg, the distance between any residential building and the near-
t public green space should not exceed 500 metres (Böhm et al. 2015, pp. 28-29).
is widely accepted that this is the distance which is easily accessible by foot for
e majority of the population (Gehl 2015, p. 143). Therefore, we propose an esti-
ate of the following indicator at the level of Hamburg's statistical areas:

Proporion of population living more than 500 metres
from the nearest public green space (> 0,5 ha)

is would allow identification of urban areas with insufficient supply of public
een spaces within the city. In order to deliver a realistic picture, the distance
ould ideally be measured within the street network, rather than being defined
 a simple buffer—considering existing spatial barriers, such as bodies of water,
ads, railways, etc.

2.1.5. Walkability

Lack of physical activity due to a sedentary lifestyle is one of the major preventab[...] health risks in Germany. Empirical evidence postulates that the proportion of phy[...] ically active people varies significantly across neighbourhoods and may correlate [...] social status. Studies suggest that socially deprived population groups tend to e[...] gage in less physical activity (Robert Koch-Institute [RKI] 2016, p. 16).

In this context, the term walkability describes a design of public open space[...] which encourages walking and thus contributes to the integration of physical a[...] tivity into the everyday life of all population groups. Hence, walkability can i[...] crease the overall quality of life in a neighbourhood, foster social interactions an[...] thus have a sustained positive impact on the physical and psychological health [...] inhabitants (Tran 2018, p. 287).

Frank et al. (2010) developed the so-called Walkability Index for comparing th[...] walkability of different urban areas, such as city districts, boroughs, neighbou[...] hoods, etc. The index encompasses four indicators: intersection density, residen[...] tial density, retail floor area ratio, and entropy. The formula used to estimate th[...] index is:

$$Walkability\text{-}Index =$$
$$(2*z\text{-}intersection\ density) + (z\text{-}residential\ density) +$$
$$(z\text{-}retail\ floor\ area\ ratio) + (z\text{-}entropy)$$

For the city of Hamburg, the defined index is computed by using statistic[...] data of household density, combined with geodata for the remaining three ind[...] cators. For the index to be included in a citywide health monitoring, however, ce[...] tain aspects must be considered. First of all, the underlying indicators and meth[...] odology must be made transparent in order to ensure an essential understandin[...] of the index while facilitating public communication of its results. Also, any ana[...] ysis should consider that the index originated in a North American spatial con[...] text. Therefore, the indicator "Retail floor area ratio" may not be applicable in th[...] context of German cities, where there are generally fewer large parking spaces i[...] commercial inner-city areas.

The Walkability Index has already been applied in a German spatial context[...] the city of Essen used it without any alterations in the methodology as part of th[...] research project "Climate Initiative Essen—Action in a New Climate Culture[...] funded by the Federal Ministry of Education and Research (Tran et al. 2017, p. 20[...] Nonetheless, we recommend carrying out an empirical study in different Germa[...] or other European cities in order to test the relevance of the indicator "Retail floc[...] area ratio" for the assessment of walkability in the European spatial realm.

2.1.6. Healthcare

Access to healthcare is particularly important for a supportive, health-promotin[...] urban living environment. In this regard, pharmacies are usually the first conta[...]

oint in the case of (minor) medical problems. Assessing the ac-
essibility of pharmacies can therefore provide an initial overview
existing health infrastructure at the neighbourhood level.

An accessibility analysis requires the coordinates of pharma-
y locations. These can be obtained from Open Street Map or
oogle Maps. As for the catchment area, we recommend using
oo metres as a proxy of walking distance, equivalent to the ac-
essibility analysis of public green spaces:

Proportion of population living 500 metres from the
nearest pharmacy

or a more comprehensive picture of the situation, the number
residents per pharmacy may be a useful addition. One of the
udy areas in the research project "Healthy Neighbourhoods",
r instance, only has one pharmacy located in the centre of the
eighbourhood. Although all inhabitants live within a 500-me-
e radius—thus having very convenient access—the indicator
oes not account for the population density, leaving a single
narmacy to serve over 6,000 who live in the area. Therefore, ac-
ounting for both indicators will provide a more detailed picture
the neighbourhood's public health facilities.

In Germany, pharmacies have had the freedom to open wher-
ver they like since 1958 and can thus be located anywhere, re-
ardless of local demand. Still, including the proposed indicator
population density into a health monitoring can be useful.
hus, neighbourhoods with poor access to pharmacies can be
entified and so-called *Notapotheken* (emergency pharmacies)
ay be opened (Bundesvereinigung Deutscher Apothekerver-
inde e. V. [ABDA] n.d.).

When it comes to choosing a general practitioner or a den-
st, proximity does not necessarily play the most decisive role.
evertheless, it does serve as an indication of the supply and ac-
ss to healthcare at the neighbourhood level. Documenting the
pacities of individual practices, such as the number of physi-
ans, average waiting times for (first) appointments, (tempo-
ry) freeze of admissions, etc., provides a highly detailed picture
the local situation. However, such extensive data collection is
ot feasible for the entire city. Conducting an accessibility analy-
s, on the other hand, is more realistic. To that end, the location
oordinates of the practices are needed. Currently, it is only pos-
ble to obtain this information manually from the website of
amburg's Medical Association through the integrated search
nction. A single list with the addresses of all general practi-

tioners and/or dentists is currently not accessible for research purposes. Therefore, the estimation of the proposed indicator is generally possible but very
time-consuming.

2.1.7. Access to Food, Alcohol and Tobacco

People with lower socioeconomic standing are less likely to maintain a healthy
diet. Studies show that adults as well as children living in deprived neighbourhoods tend to consume less fresh fruit and vegetables. Moreover, there appear
to be a higher concentration of fast-food restaurants in economically deprived
areas than in more affluent neighbourhoods (Fekete and Weyers 2015, pp. 197-
199).

Comparing the accessibility of fast-food restaurants and fruit and vegetable
vendors can provide some insight into the extent to which urban neighbourhoods have a health-promoting impact on the nutrition of residents. This is why
we propose the estimation of two indicators:

Proportion of population living more than 500 metres from
the nearest fruit and vegetable store
Proportion of population living within 500 metres of the
nearest fast-food restaurant

There are also social and economic factors which influence people's eating habits
such as personal preferences, family traditions, prices, choice, etc. (Fekete and Weyers 2015, pp. 201–203). Yet, carrying out a representative sample survey for the entire
city of Hamburg on a regular basis is not feasible. An accessibility analysis, on the
other hand, represents a suitable alternative solution. Open Street Map is a possible data source for obtaining the locations coordinates, as is data scraping from
Google Maps. Under these circumstances, random quality checks by means of on-
site visits are highly recommended in order to verify the data. Annual updates are
also necessary, since food service providers such as shops, restaurants, bakeries, etc.
tend to change location relatively often based on shifts in local demand.

Some researchers argue that density of alcohol and tobacco outlets may promote harmful habits of drinking and smoking, since these items are more readily
available to residents (Lipperman-Kreda et al. 2012, p. 547; Popova et al. 2009, p.
500). Therefore, the proposed indicator gives information about the extent to
which the living environment is likely to encourage the consumption of alcohol
and/or tobacco products:

Proportion of population living within 500 metres of the
nearest alcohol and tobacco outlet

In order to examine the exact implications, an in-depth empirical study in multiple
neighbourhoods is required. Nevertheless, the indicator may provide an overview
of existing patterns. The methodology for this estimation is the same as that for
measuring accessibility to pharmacies, fruit and vegetable shops and fast-food
restaurants.

2. Current Limitations

citywide, small-scale monitoring of health-related characteristics of
the urban environment will inevitably have certain limitations—since
its aim is to cover the big picture, some details must be left out. We want
to address two of the main current limitations:

Interval at which the available data is updated

Evaluation studies of noise pollution and heat load distribution are prepared by local authorities at specific time intervals. These intervals, however, do not necessarily coincide and therefore pose a challenge for establishing monitoring systems over the course of time. It is not necessary
for the monitoring to be conducted annually or biannually—but the
interval must be consistent. Ideally, all data sources for the estimation of
the indicators should be updated at the same time and at a consistent
pace, for example, every five years.

Consistency of methodology used for generating the data

At times, local authorities alter the methodology for preparing the previously mentioned evaluation studies. For instance, Hamburg's Behörde
für Umwelt und Energie (Local Authority of Environment and Energy)
commissioned a small-scale estimation of heat load distribution in 2012
and 2017 (GEO-NET Umweltconsulting GmbH 2012, p. 12; GEO-NET Umweltconsulting GmbH 2018, pp. 17–19). The way heat load was defined
and measured, however, differs in both studies—rendering it invalid for
generating data estimates of the same indicator to observe temporal
changes.

Conclusion and Outlook

Social deprivation, coupled with an unhealthy living environment, may
have serious implications for public health and life expectancy. What is
currently perceived merely as environmental load, a concentration of
multiple unfavourable environmental factors, can manifest itself as serious health consequences over the course of several years. The possible
adverse effects on human health triggered by long-term exposure to
these factors may evolve into chronic illnesses. Such a development poses the threat of far-reaching consequences, not only in social but also in
economic terms.

A citywide monitoring of health-related features in the neighbourhoods of Hamburg, compatible with the existing Social Monitoring,
may serve as a powerful instrument amidst the COVID-19 pandemic.
Long-term exposure to harmful environmental factors such as poor air
quality, high heat load, and noise pollution, may trigger chronic conditions such as reduced lung capacity, high blood pressure, or coronary
heart disease—all risk factors for developing more severe symptoms

6 The risk of developing severe symptoms of COVID-19 increases after the age of 50 (RKI 2020).

7 Males have been found to be more vulnerable than females (RKI 2020).

of the new coronavirus (RKI 2020). Data about the spatial distribution of the (potentially) affected population, combined with socio-demographic characteristics such as age[6], gender[7], and social status at the small scale could provide an initial base for identifying vulnerable groups in respect of COVID-19. Starting from there, city officials can conduct more comprehensive analyses, and thus confidently navigate the situation of general public health uncertainty.

There are ample sources of data, which could generally allow the implementation of the proposed monitoring. However, in order to ensure a reliable basis, certain considerations must be accounted for. First of all, the selection of the spatial observation level should be in line with place-specific characteristics. In the case of Hamburg, the statistical areas are the most suitable choice because of available statistical data and for reasons of consistency with the existing social monitoring system. Second, a data platform for the proposed monitoring should be established. The individual data sources must be checked for compatibility and their updating must be synchronised. To that end, the collaboration of different local authorities is required. Last, but not least, any alterations to the methodology for the generation of the underlying data must be kept to a minimum in order to ensure the reliability of monitoring developments over time.

With this in view, implementing the vision of a citywide small-scale monitoring of health-promoting and damaging features of the urban environment is a sensible and realistic next step for Hamburg. Before it is possible to set this into motion, a well-coordinated and synchronised data pool must be in place.

References

Bundesvereinigung Deutscher Apothekerverbände e. V. (n.d.). *Grundlagen für den Apothekenbetrieb*, viewed 17 December 2020, https://www.abda.de/apotheke-in-deutschland/grundlagen-fuer-den-apothekenbetrieb/.

Arndt, W-H. (2012). "Verkehrsplanung und Gesundheit: Stadtverkehr und seine gesundheitlichen Folgen." C. Böhme, C. Kliemke, B. Reimann and W. Süß ed. *Handbuch Stadtplanung und Gesundheit*. Bern.

hm, J., C. Böhme, A. Bunzel, C. Kühnau, and M. Reinke (2015). *Urbanes Grün in der doppelten Innenentwicklung*. Bonn-Bad Godesberg.

hme, C. & Köckler, H. (2018). "Umweltgerechtigkeit im städtischen Raum. Soziale Lage, Umweltqualität und Gesundheit zusammendenken." S. Baumgart, H. Köckler, A. Ritzinger and A. Rüdiger ed. *Planung für gesundheitsfördernde Städte*. Hannover.

aubach, M., A. Egorov, P. Mudu, T. Wolf, C.W. Thompson and M. Martuzzi (2017). "Effects of Urban Green Space on Environmental Health, Equity and Resilience." N. Kabisch, H. Korn, J. Stadler and A. Bonn ed. *Nature-Based Solutions to Climate Change Adaptation in Urban Areas*. Cham.

hörde für Stadtentwicklung und Wohnen (2019). *Sozialmonitoring Integrierte Stadtentwicklung*. Hamburg

hörde für Umwelt und Energie (2020). *Bodenversiegelung. Versiegelungskarten 1984, 1999, 2012 und 2017*, viewed 17 December 2020, https://www.hamburg.de/boden/135300/versiegelung/.

hörde für Umwelt und Energie (2017a). *Digitale Bodenkarte Hamburg. Versiegelung 2017*, viewed 17 December 2020, https://www.hamburg.de/content-blob/10357268/8c7fb428c37907cb3359e2c7d34ce101/data/versiegelung-2017.pdf.

hörde für Umwelt und Energie (2017b). *Gesamtstädtische Klimaanalyse. Aktualisierte Stadtklimaanalyse Hamburg 2017*, viewed 17 December 2020, https://www.hamburg.de/landschaftsprogramm/3957546/stadtklimaanalyse-hamburg-2017.

ropean Environment Agency (2019). *Environmental justice, environmental hazards and the vulnerable in European society*, viewed 17 December 2020, https://www.eea.europa.eu/publications/unequal-exposure-and-unequal-impacts/environmental-justice-environmental-hazards-and.

kete, C. & S. Weyers (2016). "Soziale Ungleichheit im Ernährungsverhalten: Befundlage, Ursachen und Interventionen." *Bundesgesundheitsblatt, Gesundheitsforschung, Gesundheitsschutz* 59.02: pp. 197–205.

rguson, M., H.E. Roberts, R.R.C. McEachan and M. Dallimer (2018). "Contrasting distributions of urban green infrastructure across social and ethno-racial groups." *Landscape and Urban Planning* 175: pp. 136–148.

ank, L.D., J.F. Sallis, B.E. Saelens, L. Leary, K. Cain, T.L. Conway and P.M. Hess (2010). "The development of a walkability index: application to the Neighborhood Quality of Life Study." *British journal of sports medicine*, 44.13: pp. 924–933.

hl, J. (2015). *Städte für Menschen*, Berlin.

O-NET Umweltconsulting GmbH (2012). *Stadtklimatische Bestandsaufnahme und Bewertung für das Landschaftsprogramm Hamburg Klimaanalyse und Klimawandelszenario 2050*, viewed 17 December 2020, https://www.hamburg.de/contentblob/3519382/b3caobd3483c0397fdf1a87ce4e1846a/data/gutachten-stadtklima.pdf.

O-NET Umweltconsulting GmbH (2018). *Analyse der klimaökologischen Funktionen und Prozesse für die Freie und Hansestadt Hamburg. Aktualisierte Klimaanalyse 2017*, viewed 17 December 2020, https://www.hamburg.de/contentblob/12360294/e9aa325cb135d94e962630c74524c627/data/d-dokumentation-klimaanalyse-2017.pdf.

ines, L. & L. Hagler (2007). "Noise pollution: a modem plague." *Southern medical journal* 100.3: pp. 287–294.

ußermann, H. (2008). "Wohnen und Quartier: Ursachen sozialräumlicher Segregation." EU. Huster, J. Boeckh and H. Mogge-Grotjahn ed. *Handbuch Armut und soziale Ausgrenzung*. Wiesbaden.

tz, K., L. Dunst and A. Walz (2018). *Klimaresiliente Stadtentwicklung: zunehmender Hitzestress in deutschen Groß- und Mittelstädten*. Berlin.

Klimeczek, H-J. (2011). "Environmental justice in the Federal State of Berlin—development and implementation of a new cross-cutting strategy." *UMID: Umwelt und Mensch—Informationsdienst* 2: pp. 18–19.

Lipperman-Kreda, S., J.W. Grube and K.B. Friend (2012). "Local tobacco policy and tobacco outlet density: Associations with youth smoking." *The Journal of adolescent health: official publication of the Society for Adolescent Medicine* 50.06: pp. 547–552.

Moscelli, G., L. Siciliani, N. Gutacker and R. Cookson (2018). "Socioeconomic inequality of access to healthcare: Does choice explain the gradient?", *Journal of health economics* 57, pp. 290–314.

Pampel, F.C., P.M. Krueger and J.T. Denney (2010). "Socioeconomic Disparities in Health Behaviors." *Annual review of sociology* 36: pp. 349–370.

Popova, S., N. Giesbrecht, D. Bekmuradov and J. Patra (2009). "Hours and days of sale and density of alcohol outlets: Impacts on alcohol consumption and damage: a systematic review." *Alcohol and alcoholism (Oxford, Oxfordshire)* 44.5: pp. 500–51.

Robert Koch-Institute (2020). *SARS-CoV-2 Steckbrief zur Coronavirus-Krankheit-2019 (COVID-19)*, viewed 16 December 2020, https://www.rki.de/DE/Content/InfAZ/N. Neuartiges_Coronavirus/Steckbrief.html.

Robert Koch-Institute (2016). *Gesundheit in Deutschland—die wichtigsten Entwicklungen. Gesundheitsberichterstattung des Bundes*. Berlin.

Sanderson, E., D. Briggs, M. Jantunen, B. Forsberg, M. Svartengren, R. rám, J. Gulliverand N. Janssen (2005). "Human exposure to transport-related air pollution." M. Krzyzanowski, B. Kuna-Dibbert and J. Schneider ed. *Health effects of transport-related air pollution*. Geneva.

Schwedler, H-U. (2008). *Leisere Kommunen: Informationen zur Umgebungslärmrichtlinie*. Berlin.

Senatsverwaltung für Stadtentwicklung und Wohnen (2019). *Bericht Monitoring Soziale Stadtentwicklung* Berlin 2019, viewed 16 December 2020, https://www. stadtentwicklung.berlin.de/planen/basisdaten_stadtentwicklung/monitoring/ de/2019/index.shtml.

Tran, M-C. (2018). "Walkability als ein Baustein gesundheitsförderlicher Stadtentwicklung und -gestaltung." S. Baumgart, H. Köckler, A. Ritzinger and A. Rüdiger ed. *Planung für gesundheitsfördernde Städte*. Hannover.

Tran, M-C., C. Manz and F. Nouri (2017). "Messung und Erfassung der Fußgängerfreundlichkeit von Stadträumen. Eine GIS-basierte Analyse gemischt genutzter Quartiersgebiete am Fallbeispiel Essen mit Hilfe des integrierten Walkability Audits auf Mikroebene (IWAM)" *Institut für Stadtplanung und Städtebau*. Universität Duisburg-Essen.

Yosifova, E. & J. Pohlan (2021). "Umwelt- und Umgebungsmerkmale von Quartieren mit unterschiedlicher sozialer Lage." J. Westenhöfer, S. Busch, J. Pohlan, O. von dem Knesebeck and E. Swart ed. *Gesundheitsförderung und Prävention im städtischen Kontext*. Hamburg.

7. Advancing Participatory Democracy through Collaborative Data Platforms

Rosa Thoneick/Till Degkwitz/Claudius Lieven

Introduction

This paper investigates the argument that facilitating open data for democratic processes requires a transformation of the underlying processes as well as a strong functional integration into participatory systems. The evolution from conventional planning to its digitisation is not solely a technological shift, but necessitates fundamental procedural changes (Silva 2010). This requires broadening the scope in planning digitisation beyond the use of technical tools to include an analysis of the respective context (Kubicek 2010).

This research analyses two tools, developed in Hamburg, for digital urban participation by highlighting their core characteristics, addressing shortcomings, and discussing possible improvements. Knowledge from an examination of local case studies, including European and Asian examples, reveals insights that are valuable for introducing and intensifying the use of urban data in pursuit of participatory models of democracy.

Urban Data Hub and Digital Participation System

In 2015 the Senate of Hamburg released a strategy document intended to pave the way for the digital city. By relating a smart city narrative, the initiative laid the foundation for two ongoing collaborative projects; (1) the Urban Data Hub (UDH) as a cooperation, a project between the HafenCity University CityScienceLab (CSL) and the Agency for Geoinformation and Surveying (LGV); together with (2) the Digital Participation System (DIPAS) developed by the Administration for Urban Development and Housing (BSW) in cooperation with the CSL and the Agency for Geoinformation and Surveying. The authors worked in these projects as researchers, developers and project coordinators.

The Urban Data Hub is an organisational unit consulting on matters of technology, services, interfaces, and formats, while investigating development needs regarding urban data in Hamburg. It also operates and develops the Urban Data Platform (UDP). This platform publishes open-source data, making it freely available to citizens and stakeholders as well as to government administrations. It aims to enhance the public's accessibility to data; to foster the reuse of public data; promote evidence-based decision-making in urban planning; and create a well-informed public that, at best, can monitor the city's urban development. The Urban Data Hub further improves data comprehensibility by introducing analytical tools and data visualisations to the platform. This article, therefore, focuses on the platform's capacity for citizen accessibility via web-based, geographic information systems (GIS) as the primary interface. Although the city of Hamburg has an open data portal, this will not be explored further in the following discussion.

DIPAS, the Digital Participation System, is the result of an extensive series of local participation projects carried out throughout Hamburg. As a cooperation project between the BSW, LGV and the CityScienceLab, the objective of DIPAS is to develop, test, and implement a digital workshop tool to be used for physical participation workshops, building on a prevailing online participation platform. It combines a workshop tool developed within the "FindingPlaces Project" at HafenCity University (Noyman et al. 2017) with an online participation tool from the *Stadtwerkstatt* (urban workshop). As an administrative institution, *Stadtwerkstatt* coordinates informal citizen participation in regards to topics of urban planning and environment in Hamburg (Lieven 2017). Both tools utilise web-based interfaces, and are accessible by a variety of devices, allowing citizens to participate either online, from a computer or smartphone, or onsite, in participatory events via digital workshop tool. The digital workshop tool then displays citizen comments, maps, and georeferenced data on a large touch screen application. This browser-based application an extension of an existing online participation tool. The graphical user interface comprises an interactive map displaying georeferenced data, alongside input features collecting user contributions and other functionalities such as commentary

nd filtering options. With this, citizens can access geospatial information, discuss
ith planners onsite, while commenting on the suggestions of others. These activi-
es, contributions and comments are then made accessible to planners. DIPAS is
herefore classified as a softGIS tool in its visualisation of localised experiential
nowledge through user-friendly interfaces (Kyttä et al. 2011).

he UDH and the DIPAS are both crucial projects of the digital infrastructure in
amburg; however, they are only partly accessible to the general public. One pro-
des essential information on demographics, education, infrastructure, etc., while
e other establishes online participation to allow for web-based democratic pro-
sses. Although the foundation of their functionalities was established over the
ast few years, their tools have yet to be fully developed in order to facilitate two
asic democratic processes, as established by Meijer (2012).

ree Levels of Democratic Processes

emocratic processes can be understood as distinguished by the three intercon-
ected levels elucidated by Meijer (2012): monitorial, deliberative, and participatory.
 monitorial model of democracy considers citizens as watchful, well-informed
gents, with the role of holding government accountable. Governments in monito-
al democracies extensively publish an extensive range of information in order to
nsure an informed citizenry. A proactive interpretation of this model is that data
atforms offer the digital infrastructure for conveying crucial information to the
eneral public.

 an extensive deliberative democracy open debate is crucial to finding collective
lutions to public problems (Meijer 2012). Citizens are discussants and deliberate
oout actions and decisions made by the government—in doing so, they indirectly
ert influence on actions and decision-making. Governments in deliberative demo-
acies invite citizens to share and present their perspectives, providing (e.g. online)
ols that foster engagement and public debate. Therefore open-data discussion
atforms stimulate conversation and dialogue horizontally—meaning between
tizens, as well as vertically—from citizens to government.

 the third level, the participatory democracy, the active engagement of citizens is
icouraged, while collaboration is employed to find solutions to public challenges
eijer 2012; Ruijer et al. 2017). As collaborators in the decision-making process, citi-
ns become co-creators of public policy, transforming the role of government from
rvice provider to partner. Open data platforms in participatory democracies facil-
ate the interaction and collaboration of citizens, civil society, and businesses—to-
ther with governmental organisations. The platforms become a critical collabora-
on tool for cultivating participation in collective decision-making efforts.

UDP, DIPAS and their Democratic Depth

The research applies the three-tiered democracy model as established by Meijer and Ruijer to the urban context of Hamburg, analysing the Urban Data Platform and Digital Participation System. Taking into account that the analysis is based on model description of the two projects, the description is of a best-case scenario. However, in several pilot events, usability and user experience studies, development potentialities were revealed which are elaborated on in the subsequent chapter.

Since "the role of government in a monitorial democratic process is to disclose information" (Meijer 2012, p. 2), the UDP plays the role of a central government tool proactively informing citizens themselves, and monitors the impact of public policies. This monitorial use of public sector information is legislated for in Hamburg's transparency law (§1 Section 1 HmbTG). The provision of information allows citizens to actively gather knowledge about government performance, and monitor the mandate to rule. It can be assumed that data preselection is subject to the influences of political agendas and power structures—hence, never entirely objective (Kitchin et al. 2016). It is then crucial to provide functionalities for data analytic which are publicly available. As corresponding features are being tested at the internal stage (Senate of Hamburg 2020), the UDP GIS data visualisation is assessed as an open data tool able to facilitate a monitorial relationship between citizens and the public administration. Preselected data is depicted in charts or dashboards, synthesised with other data sources, and presented with the aim of reducing complexity while maximising insights.

In a deliberative democracy, a central function of government is to invite citizens to express their views on public issues. Open data platforms can strengthen this process by "creating a level playing field for all participants in the public debate. Government-coordinated platforms examine every suggestion and give precise feedback on why certain ideas, or parts of it can or cannot be implemented" (Ruijer et al. 2017, p. 2). In the case of DIPAS, the platform facilitates public discussions by providing citizens with access to georeferenced planning information via the visual workshop tool. The tool is thus offering opportunities for levelling the knowledge gap between citizens and those managing planning procedures. DIPAS further invites citizens to voice their opinion via a contribution form. All contributions are then visually mapped on the publicly accessible platform, while enabling virtual discussions by comment functions. Thus, the platform assures transparency in participation procedures, while strengthening deliberations within the community and between citizens and government.

Shortcomings of UDP and DIPAS

Both UDP and DIPAS have extensive potential for improving monitorial and deliberative democratic processes in Hamburg. However, findings derived from the

search of the UDP application, together with piloting and usability studies con-
ucted throughout the project runtime of DIPAS, show that both tools currently fall
ort of exploiting their full potential.

order to establish the UDP as a central digital tool to foster monitorial democrat-
processes, certain technological advances are necessary. Open data platforms
ust provide data visualisation functionalities in order to enable user insights,
ntent interpretations, and discussion engagements (Bohman 2015; Malandrino et
2016; Pirozzi and Scarano 2016). Although the web GIS interface of the UDP is ad-
nced compared with traditional open data portals that mostly offer data ar-
iving and downloading options (European Commission 2020), it continues to lack
veral crucial features.

other shortcoming of the UDP is its topicality and a general lack of public aware-
ss. For the city of Hamburg, demographic data is not regularly updated, and only
ailable at the district level; however, neither smaller administrative entities nor
storical data are accessible (Landesbetrieb Geoinformation und Vermessung
20). Even though the UDP has around 10–15 million calls per month (Urban Data
atform Cockpit 2020) and an average of 115 thousand visitors, there is virtually no
blic awareness or news coverage about the platform or the data it provides.
ijer et al. (2017) consider the media a crucial intermediary between citizens and
vernment officials; therefore, a lack of coverage may indicate a lack of public dis-
urse, with possible adverse effects on monitorial effectiveness.

a participatory democracy, collaborative partnerships between citizens and gov-
nmental organisations are integral for taking part in decision-making processes
uijer et al. 2017). Although DIPAS facilitates deliberative practices and the involve-
ent of citizens, it does not provide options for informed decision-making by citi-
ns. Up to now, the legal regulations on citizen participation have only provided
fensive rights to protect against state intervention in private property. The crea-
e participation of citizens in planning processes is limited to participation in the
rmulation of the objectives of planning processes and consultation on alterna-
e solutions. The decision on the planning solution is reserved for democratically
gitimised bodies (Behörde für Stadtentwicklung und Umwelt 2013). This results in
ragmented participation reality, where the extent of citizen involvement varies
m the commitment and capacities of one planning authority to another. As has
en stated above, this is an example of where the scope of planning digitisation
uld be broadened to include the planning context beyond the tool.

rrently, guidelines for initiating and implementing participation processes do
t account for the treatment of results. This chronic failure of not having a proce-
re for handling the results of participation processes weakens their credibility,

hence the term "Particitainment" (in reference to a saturation of participation in tiatives) was coined by Klaus Selle (2011). In evaluations of user experience studie citizens express scepticism about the extent to which their input has real impac One reason for this deficit is, as already mentioned, the lack of a legislative fram work. Another is the perceived black-box interpretation of the results. This is n specific to DIPAS but a broader phenomenon in the context of participation proc dures: rather than focus on tools and methodologies, participation must be r searched with contextual considerations, while examining the governmental cor mitment to the embedded tools.

Another aspect is the rupture in planning processes—both in terms of a changir public that participates, and a perceived fragmentation. An obstacle to comprehe sive public monitoring of urban planning project is the extended time periods r quired for their development, in addition to demanding an overview of diverse i formation sources and stakeholders.

Towards more Democratic Tools

Taking into consideration the above mentioned shortcomings, suggestions for ir provements for optimising the performance of the platforms, in respect of the d liberative and participatory democratic models, are elaborated. The research pr poses an extensive integration and provision of tools, alongside a set of technic developments.

Pirozzi and Scarano (2016) observe that a shortfall of many open data portals is a insufficient functionality regarding usability, informativeness and understandab ities—hence, reducing their explorative potential. This calls for a further integratio of comprehensive public features for data analytics and visualisation. To unlea the full potential of the platform, functionalities such as "data storytelling (narr tive visualisation), infographics (viral visualisation), data physicalisation (physic visualisation), and the quantified self (personal visualisation)" (Bohman 2015, p. 31 must be included. As Ruijer et al. (2017) points out, the role of citizens in a monitor al democracy is to scrutinise government performance. To enable users of a pla form to properly analyse and oversee government objectives and policies, larg quantities of historical data need to be made available (Sousa et al. 2010). Keepir the data meticulously updated, under privacy policies, and including historic data, is critical for the monitorial capabilities of the platform. The proposed exte sions stem from the assumption that "the success of open data systems, to a grea extent, depends on the use and quality of the data provided" (Janssen et al. 201 p.266).

Parallel to this extension, we propose a complete integration of DIPAS and UDH a well as a commoning of DIPAS. This includes three aspects regarding data, analyt l features, and open-source code. First, a commoning of DIPAS presupposes that data gathered in participatory processes is published as open data. Second, the orementioned analytical features are fully supported in DIPAS to foster evi-ence-based discussions. This proposes functionalities allowing contributions to be underlined or amended by depiction of customised charts or data stories. Finally, PAS—or the DIPAS-UDH hybrid—is opened for public accessibility, enabling citi-ns, civil society, and stakeholders to engage in participatory processes while also ing the platform for their personal agendas and professional work.

is results in an online platform cultivating the formation of public opinion, sup-orted by various open data sources, while ensuring monitorial functionalities as a undation of the process. A technical intersection between the UDH and the public uthority's planning system currently implements these suggestions by integrat-g data sets gathered during participation processes. Data are provided by the DH, by use of additional geographical information in a participatory project. Sim-arly, data gathered in DIPAS processes were, at times, temporarily published as en data via the corresponding platform. Preparations for an open-source pub-hing of DIPAS were underway during the writing of this article.

hy Merging Alone Doesn't Do the Trick

a participatory democracy, citizens actively collaborate and engage in solving ublic challenges, while governments offer a collaborative environment that en-les this collective decision-making (Ruijer et al. 2017). In this light, institutional mmitments need to be prioritised and re-assessed, shifting focus to communities nd cooperative processes. Possible vantage points are integrating data gathered om informal participation into formalised participation procedures, to ensure a gher coherence and uptake of citizen data, thus cultivating communities of partic-ation.

pursuit of participatory democratic processes, a culture and institutionalisation open government, alongside the provision of instruments and tools, must be urtured (Janssen et al. 2012). While digitisation alone cannot tackle the legal amework, there is significant room for improving the handling and storing of citi-n data. In order to deduce citizen demands and suggestions, while managing the se in data corresponding to the increase in application and use of digital partici-ation tools, DIPAS started developing NLP (Natural Language Processing) based aluation tools for citizen contributions (Lieven et al. 2021). In addition to a simpli-ation of the process, it aims to achieve uniform, transparent, and unbiased evalu-ions of citizen contributions. This strengthens the validity of participation results, us promoting their integration into the implementation of urban plans.

tegrating digital participation tools and mechanisms into processes of urban development anticipates the creation of a database equipped with local knowledge about a given city. An aggregated and machine-learning facilitated evaluation then identifies thematic and sub-spatial problems and preferences. The empirical findings, as derived from a variety of contributions, are introduced into the planning and design process as empirically sound citizen suggestions. The tools generated by incorporating these suggestions are valuable for democratic procedures. The weight aggregated by countless citizen contributions over an extended period of time has the potential to exert considerable influence on processes that shape decisions.

Several other cities have established platforms and permanent discussion boards aiming to nurture a more profound discourse between users and a stronger identification with participation tools. In Spain, Madrid's Decide platform and Barcelona's Decidim use "computational features, such as discussion threads, scoring, ranking, file sharing (e.g., texts and videos), event coordination, thematic clustering and visualisation, notifications about issues or themes, and the ability of users to follow content and other users, to create a digital space where citizens deliberate and directly decide on proposals, budgets, and plans for their city" (Smith and Martín 2020). In particular, the ability to follow other users and content opens possibilities for creating communities of participation that allow a sustained discourse to align planning processes.

One condition for successfully applying citizen intelligence platforms is assuring the transparency of source data, their processing, and the suggestions derived from them. To guarantee this, the code and the algorithms must be open-source, ensuring the traceability of data evaluation. Absolute transparency prevents assumed manipulation, or even manipulation itself. The above mentioned Spanish *Decide* and *Decidim* platforms, along with the Taiwanese platforms, follow this logic. The Taiwanese platforms demonstrate how such government efficiency can be boosted while promoting broader participation in public affairs (Jung 2019). In Taiwan, besides the annual presidential hackathons, electronic democracy substantially impacts policy-making (Hierlemann 2020). The spectrum of topics which are consulted range from legislation to taxation and from education, to planning. For general or national issues, digital participation has become crucial for generating political legitimacy of citizen-sourced recommendations. The example of Taiwan proves that political legitimacy can be nurtured through massive digital citizen participation.

With this in mind, crowdsourcing can encourage citizens to co-produce knowledge and actively participate in the creation of urban data. Their insights and observations can complement, specify, and possibly offer corrections to the expertise of public authorities in their management of urban processes. Over the past few

ars, various applications have been developed to enable millions of citizens in dif-
rent countries to become active co-creators of their societies, directly taking part
democractic processes. However, these remain isolated instances, while the
ajority of citizens have yet to hear of these tools and the opportunities they offer.
pivot factor for the success of digital participation tools and urban data plat-
rms is their anchoring for the everyday use of social information, deliberation,
id decision-making. In order to disseminate these platforms it is crucial to im-
rove their visibility and topicality.

addressing technical adjustments, in addition to localising digital participation
ols, this paper aims to inspire future analyses of citizen engagement and commu-
cation with public administrations, to explore the influence of public engage-
ent on planning processes. The authors contend that of critical importance to an
nplementation of the proposed changes in Hamburg is political will and a reas-
ssment of priorities in terms of constitutional commitment. These changes are
eemed necessary and a government commitment to greater democracy in the
gital space is overdue.

References

Behörde für Stadtentwicklung und Umwelt (2013). *Hamburg gemeinsam gestalten*. Hamburg.

Bohman, S. (2015). "Data Visualization: An Untapped Potential for Political Participation and Civic Engagement." A. Kö and E. Francesconi ed. *Electronic government and the information systems perspective: 4th international conference, EGOVIS 2015, Valencia, Spain, September 1–3, 2015 proceedings*. Cham.

European Commission (2020). *European Data Portal—Recommendations for Open Data Portals: from setup to sustainability*. Luxembourg.

Hierlemann, D. (2020). "Digital Democracy: What Europe can learn from Taiwan." *Bertelsmann Stiftung, Gütersloh. 2020 Archive of European Integration*, viewed 20 October 2020, http://aei.pitt.edu/id/eprint/103223.

Janssen, M., Y. Charalabidis and A. Zuiderwijk (2012). "Benefits, Adoption Barriers and Myths of Open Data and Open Government." *Information Systems Management* 29.4: pp. 258–268.

Jung, Y. H. (2019). "The Inspiration from Open Government, Public Engagement and Agile Governance: A Case Study of Tax E-filing System Reform in Taiwan. *Conference Paper at the 27th NISPAcee Annual Conference 2019*. Prague.

Kubicek, H. (2010). "The Potential of E-Participation in Urban Planning." C.N. Silva ed. *Handbook of Research on E-Planning. IGI Global, Lisbon* pp. 168–194.

Kyttä, A. M, A. K. Broberg and M.H. Kahila (2012). "Urban environment and children's active lifestyle: softGIS revealing children's behavioral patterns and meaningful places." *American journal of health promotion AJHP* 26.5: pp 137–48.

Landesbetrieb Geoinformation und Vermessung Geo-Online. Viewed 09 January 2020, https://geoportal-hamburg.de/geo-online/. Accessed 9/1/2020.

Lieven, C. (2017). "DIPAS—Towards an integrated GIS-based system for civic participation." *Procedia Computer Science* 112: pp. 2473–2485.

Lieven C., B. Lüders, D. Kulus, R. Thoneick (2021). "Enabling Digital Co-creation in Urban Planning and Development." A. Zimmermann, R. Howlett, and L. Jain ed. *Human Centred Intelligent Systems. Smart Innovation, Systems and Technologies* 198. Singapore.

Malandrino, D., G. Cordasco, I.E. Manno et al. (2016). "An Architecture for Social Sharing and Collaboration around Open Data Visualisations." D. Gergle, M.R. Morris, P. Bjørn, and J. Konstan ed. *Proceedings of the 19th ACM Conference on Computer Supported Cooperative Work and Social Computing Companion— CSCW '16 Companion*. New York.

Meijer, AJ. (2012). "The Do It Yourself State." *Information Polity* 17.3,4: pp. 303–314.

Noyman, A., T. Holtz, J. Kröger, JR. Noennig and K. Larson (2017). "Finding Places: HCI Platform for Public Participation in Refugees' Accommodation Process." *Procedia Computer Science* 112: pp. 2463–2472.

Pirozzi, D. and V.Scarano (2016). "Support Citizens in Visualising Open Data." IEEE Computer Society ed. *20th International Conference Information Visualisation (IV)*. IEEE. pp. 271–276.

Ruijer, E., S. Grimmelikhuijsen and A. Meijer (2017). "Open data for democracy: Developing a theoretical framework for open data use." *Government Information Quarterly* 34.1: pp. 45–52.

Senate of Hamburg (2015). *Die Digitalisierung der großen Stadt—Chancen für Wirtschaftskraft, Kommunikation und öffentliche Dienstleistungen*.

enate of Hamburg (2020). *Digitale Stadt*. Hamburg.

elle, K. (2011). *"Particitainment"—oder: Beteiligen wir uns zu Tode?* PND online III, viewed 14 October 2020, http://www.planung-neu-denken. de/images/ stories/pnd/dokumente/3_2011/selle_particitainment.pdf.

ilva, C.N. (ed). (2010). *Handbook of Research on E-Planning*. IGI Global, Lisbon.

mith, A. & P. Martín (2020). "Going Beyond the Smart City? Implementing Tech-nopolitical Platforms for Urban Democracy in Madrid and Barcelona." *Journal of Urban Technology* 22.8: pp. 1–20.

ousa, A.A., P. Agante, and L.B. Gouveia (2010). "Governmeter: Monitoring Gov-ernment Performance. A Web Based Application Proposal." K.N. Andersen, E. Francesconi, Å. Grönlund, and T.M. van Engers ed. *Electronic Government and the Information Systems Perspective*. Berlin, Heidelberg.

Future and the city

. Of Zeros and Ones: Choices That Shape the Zero Carbon and Digital City of Tomorrow

Nikita John/Lisa Harseim/Gionatan Vignola/ Cathrin Zengerling

etting the Scene

the goal of the Paris Agreement of mitigating global tempera-
ure rise by 2 Celsius° is to be taken seriously and implemented
ncrementally, it is necessary to reduce per capita CO2 emissions
o 2tCO2e/cap/y by 2050[1]. In Hamburg, the city estimates that the
verage resident has a carbon footprint of about 9tCO2/cap/y.[2]
eaching the reduction goal of the Paris Agreement therefore re-
uires fundamental changes in urban infrastructures and life-
:yles. The "Urban Footprints" research project explores modes of
rban governance coping with this challenge in an accountable
nanner, by analysing eight international cities, including Ham-
urg (Zengerling 2018). In an experimental endeavour, the work-
nop "Urbanites Without Footprints" was hosted at the 2019 City
cience Summit "Cities Without" organized by the HCU *City-
:ienceLab* in cooperation with the MIT Media Lab, at HafenCity
niversity Hamburg. Participants were challenged to a *dérive*—
:epping into the role of three different urbanite avatars, each
presenting a different socio-economic group. Their daily life was
ocumented by the creation of mental maps, with particular focus
n housing, mobility, and food supply[3]. Is it possible to live in the
afenCity without the trace of a carbon footprint—in a district
pecifically designed and planned in pursuit of sustainable life-
:yles?

1 This is also the per capita goal
set in the 2015 Hamburg Climate
Plan (City of Hamburg 2015, p. 13)

2 With 9tCO2/cap/y Hamburg reached
its per capita goal for 2020 already in
2017. However, so far Hamburg only
accounts for CO2 emissions and no
other GHGs (City of Hamburg 2017)

3 The choice of sector was based
on Pichler et al. 2017, pp. 1–11

PROFILE ⟶ CONSUMPTION PATTERN ⟶		**Anne** 25 y.o. Student / Low Income / Environmentally conscious 19 sq.m	**Karen** 35 y.o. Teacher / Middle Income Family Oriented 60 sq. m.	**Stefan** 45 y.o. Businessman / High Income Health Conscious 100 sq. m.
HOUSING	Heat Consumption	★☆☆	★★☆	★★★
	Green Energy	★☆☆	★★☆	★★★
	Electricity Consumption	★☆☆	★★☆	★★★
MOBILITY	Cycling	★★★	★☆☆	★★☆
	Public Transport	★★★	★★☆	★☆☆
	Private Transport	★☆☆	★★☆	★★★
	Intercontinental Air Travel	★☆☆	★★☆	★★★
NUTRITION	Plant-Based Diet	★★★	★☆☆	★☆☆
	Regional Produce	★☆☆	★★★	★☆☆
	Organic Produce	★☆☆	★★☆	★★★
	Processed Food	★☆☆	★★☆	★★★

The urbanites' choices, as illustrated in the table above, are determined by a realistic combination of their personal and economic interests.

The following is an essayistic vision of the future, addressing the megatrends of low-carbon development and digitalisation based on insights gained during the City Science Summit workshop. The interaction between individual choices (demand) and urban planning (supply) are considered, while exploring possibilities of both utopian and dystopian features.

Stepping Into The Vision for 2050

The urbanites are hyper-equipped with knowledge of the city available low-carbon choices, supported by intuitive interfaces which employ real-time, interactive, and visually augmented information about reality (Bühling et al. 2012)—all designed to reveal traditionally hidden carbon footprints[4]. Drones, as descendants of the primary *Unmanned Aerial Vehicles*, have an equal share in the regulated airspace and are programmed to monitor the city. They are credited with increasing the efficiency of traffic control while contributing to a reduction in urban crime. Digitalisation allows swifter and more focused planning—of citizens and the city alike, unleashing unused potential while maximising human well-being, by reducing everything to a formula calculation. This is a day in the life of the urbanites ...

4 These can be better recognised through tools like the Carbon Footprint Calculator (Umweltbundesamt 2019) which was also used to create relevant profiles for Anne, Karen and Stefan

HOUSING		MOBILITY		NUTRITION	
Smart Heat Meter	Community Housing	Mass Transport Bonus	Autonomous Rideshare	Vertical Farming	Food Management App
★☆☆	★★★	★★★	★☆☆	★☆☆	★★★

nne starts her day with a pre-packaged, nutrient-rich breakfast designed to pro-
de a balanced diet at an affordable price—attributes, which its fresh counterparts
nnot provide. Using mass transport she reaches the office, adding to her *Bonus*
ith every trip. During lunch, she gets an overview of the offers at the *Vertico Farm*
permarket, offering fresh, organic, and local products, by means of her *Food
anagement App*. Today, *Vertico Farm* has nothing she is willing to pay for. Instead,
er *Food-Share App* notifies her that User:*Stephano2* has salad to give away, while
ser:*Mamabear* baked too many *Nussecken* (typical German pastry) for a party and
fers the leftovers in a community forum. That day, Anne works over-time, so her
am leader offers to pay her autonomous rideshare, a luxury she cannot usually
ford. She sold her bike after the roads were transformed into the statistically safer
tonomous rideshare lanes.

nce the city centre is now exclusively reserved for community housing, she reaches
ome just in time for dinner in the shared kitchen, even making arrangements to
orrow the neighbour's canoe for the weekend. With her exceptionally low heating
ll notification, she is awarded one bulk purchase coupon for the *Vertico Farm* super-
arket, which, however, is too much food unless her community wants to utilise it.

	HOUSING			MOBILITY			NUTRITION	
Smart Heat Meter	Community Housing		Mass Transport Bonus	Autonomous Rideshare		Vertical Farming	Food Management App	
★ ★ ★	★ ★ ☆		★ ★ ☆	★ ★ ☆		★ ★ ☆	★ ★ ★	

Karen is checking out the fresh and local organic food on offer at *Vertico Farm* o her *Food Management App*, while sipping a cup of morning tea. She uploads he shopping list, and the app advises her that some of the grocery items are slight over budget. The building in which she lives is designated for working families, s she can send her son Elias off to the kindergarten in the autonomous e-carpoc managed by the parents in the neighbourhood.

Her daily heating bill notification appears, which is regulated by the housin community's smart meters. She receives praise for being extraordinarily carefu with her energy use this month and is awarded a supermarket voucher. After ba ancing her shopping list with her budget, she heads out using mass transpo which is more efficient than walking and gives her the benefit of stocking up on he *Bonus* points. She doesn't care much for rideshares, with the exception of the neigl bourhood carpool, which is a good way to stay connected with the other parents i the community.

While on the train to work, she takes the initiative to share her leftover *Nussecke* from the weekly community dinner on the supermarket's *Food-Share App*. Her con munity members, who also babysit Elias when the couple works late, hand over th extra *Nussecken* to a student who drops by at the end of the day.

HOUSING		MOBILITY		NUTRITION	
Smart Heat Meter	Community Housing	Mass Transport Bonus	Autonomous Rideshare	Vertical Farming	Food Management App
★☆☆	★★☆	★☆☆	★★★	★★★	★★★

efan walks from his lavish living space onto his private balcony, which he can
ford after certifying his home as energy positive. His work no longer involves
mmuting to the city centre during rush-hour, since executive decisions are now
ade in VR-boardrooms. Therefore, living outside of the centre doesn't affect his
ily life. He still keeps his old-timer, modified to run on biofuel, for the few luxuri-
us weekend drives through the countryside, since driving within city limits is pro-
bited due to its environmental inefficiency.

His feed for premium nutrition advice, synced to the *Food Management App*, in-
cates that he is in need of foods rich in B12. He adds shellfish from the *Vertico Farms*
uaponic system to his weekly shopping basket, enhancing his benefits as a loyal
stomer. As he steps out, he notices discarded protest placards accusing him, and
s neighbours living in *Zimt Tower*, of using excessive heating energy for their spa-
us homes. The energy company insists that the only information they released
as for motivating the low-energy neighbourhoods—and that they did not leak any
nfidential information about residents. Stefan does not feel guilty, since he is con-
ually reminded, assured, and rewarded for his low carbon rating. While waiting
r his rideshare, his *Food Management App* asks if he would like to put his four-day-
d lettuce up for sharing. He accepts with a swipe to the right.

The Transition from 2020 to the 2050 Planner

The future described above depicts constant citizen engage ment with the help of digitally collected ratings. Planners, how ever, do not act solely based on ratings, but rather as active me diators. They can choose between rating systems (Sparling ar Sen 2011) as complementary to services, with the capacity t gauge algorithms used for the translation of data, compl menting both the cumulative needs of urban citizens and a counting for planetary boundaries.

The urban planning decision of 2020, which specified that the should be only community living in the city centre, ensured affor able housing for everyone, with the inclusion of a social aspect ar the implementation of family-focused areas. The compulsory int gration of smart heating meters ensures that residential co sumption of energy is regulated, while also functioning as a pr motional tool for steering consumption habits. Initially, th phasing out of private homes and landownership was met wit strong resistance. However, these traditional ways of living a slowly losing popularity as a result of the high maintenan costs. Instead, planners now tackle traces of "digital homeles ness" and gentrification tied to housing application responses.

What had initially started as a last-mile connection, *Auton mous Rideshare* eventually took over urban transport (Creutz et al. 2019, p.5) due to the pressures from private companie Public planners also gave in to private companies in their pu suit of upgrading the city's cycling infrastructure—since th company plans had a higher resolution owing to mobility-da marketplaces (WBGU 2019, p.60), efficient streamlining wit better monitoring capability of logistics and freight, as well lower accident risks and long-term emissions (ibid. p.67).

steep decline in the use of private vehicles freed up parking areas (Creutzig et al. 2019, p.60) in the inner city, complementing the commuter trains, which further gained in popularity amongst urbanites with the introduction of the *CO2 Bonus*. Urbanites are now beginning to donate user data (WBGU 2019, p.60), as planners focus on creating more robust systems with improved cybersecurity (Holmes 2020) along with data and liability policies (WBGU 2019, p.60). So, there remains the possibility of salvaging cycling and using waterways for daily transport, while restoring a sense of safety amongst urbanites.

The *Food Management App*, coordinating between the urbane-driven food sharing function (Foodwaste 2019), fridge feed, and nutrition watch, improves the overview of demand in the city, while minimising waste on the consumption side. Additionally, *Vertico Farm* contributes significantly to the reduction of environmental impacts associated with packaging and logistics (WBGU 2019, p.60), synthesising digital farming (Shchutskaya, et al. 2019, pp. 269–279) with optimised urban and peri-urban land use by making use of the *Food Management App*. Trustworthy open-source blockchain and DLC data systems inform and support local organic farmers (WBGU 2019, p.14), in so, contributing to the vision created by the UN Sustainable Development Goals—albeit without accounting for the looming threat posed by multinational agricultural corporations (see Despommier 2011).

Voices that Shape the City

The megatrends of low-carbon development and digitalisation pose complex challenges for societies at a local and global scale. The so-called *smart city* describes a sustainable and equitable city, resulting from the overabundance and integration of data, reinforced by automated and algorithmic mechanisms of decision-making. These promises of digitalisation, however come with real risks (Bauriedl & Strüver 2018, p.11): the loss of privacy from around-the-clock surveillance; replacement of transparent and conscious value judgments with algorithmic biases; the loss of democratic decision-making on former public and now privatised services and infrastructures; and vulnerabilities and rebound-effects of ICT "solutions", whose production is often energy and material intensive (Saxe 2019). Therefore it is crucial for urbanites, planners, and researchers alike to critically question

smart city agendas (Späth and Knieling 2018, pp. 347–358), an
(re)consider "dumb" city approaches (Saxe 2019) in the pursuit c
low-carbon and equitable cities on a human scale (see Gehl 201
BMUB 2017).

References

BMUB (2017). *Smart City Charta*, viewed 03 April 2021, https://www.bmi.bund.de/
SharedDocs/downloads/DE/veroeffentlichungen/themen/bauen/wohnen/smart
city-charta-langfassung.pdf;jsessionid=C088FA93ADBE3B0EA873AFDB-
6B242E19.2_cid364?__blob=publicationFile&v=7.

Bühling, R., M. Obaid, S. Hammer, and E. André (2012). "Mobile augmented reality
and adaptive art: a game-based motivation for energy saving." *11th Internatio.
al Conference on Mobile and Ubiquitous Multimedia*. Ulm, Germany, viewed 03
April 2021, https://doi.org/10.1145/2406367.2406428.

City of Hamburg (2015). *Hamburg Climate Plan: Report by the Senate to the
Hamburg Parliament*, viewed 03 April 2021, https://www.hamburg.de/content
blob/9051304/754a498fcf4e4bbf9516e1f9a99e2bfe/data/
d-21-2521-hamburg-climate-plan.pdf.

City of Hamburg (2017). *CO2 emissions in Hamburg: Balance Sheet of the North Statistics Office for 2017*, viewed 03 April 2021, https://www.hamburg.de/
co2-bilanz-hh/.

Despommier, D. (2011). *The Vertical Farm: Feeding the World in the 21st Century*.
New York.

Gehl, J. (2013). *Cities for People*. Washington D.C..

Holmes, A. (2020). "An artist wheeled 99 smartphones around in a wagon to create
fake traffic jams on Google Maps." *Business Insider*, viewed 03 April 2021,
https://www.businessinsider.de/international/google-maps-traffic-jam-99-
smartphones-wagon-2020-2/?r=US&IR=T.

Pichler, P.P., T. Zwickel, A. Chavez, T. Kretschmer, J. Seddon and H. Weisz (2017).
"Reducing urban greenhouse gas footprints." *Scientific Reports* 7.1: pp.1–11.

Saxe, S. (2019). "I'm an Engineer, I am not buying into 'smart' cities." *New York Time*
16 Jul., viewed 03 April 2021, https://www.nytimes.com/2019/07/16/opinion/
smart-cities.html.

Shchutskaya, A., E. Afanaseva, and L. Kapustina (2019). "Digital farming development in Russia: Regional aspects." *Digital Transformation of the Economy—
Challenges, Trends and New Opportunities* pp.269–279.

Sparling, E.I and S. Sen (2011). "Rating: How Difficult is It?" *Fifth ACM conference on
Recommender Systems*. Chicago.

äth, P. and J. Knieling (2018). "Endlich Smart-City-Leuchtturm: Auswirkungen des EU-Projektes mySMARTLife auf die Planungspraxis in Hamburg." S. Bauriedl and A. Strüver ed. *Smart City—Kritische Perspektiven auf die Digitalisierung in Städten*. Bielefeld.

nweltbundesamt (2019). *CO2-Rechner: Carbon Footprint Calculator,* viewed 03 April 2021, https://uba.co2-rechner.de/de_DE/.

3GU (2019). *Towards our common digital future: WBGU Flagship Report*. Berlin, viewed 03 April 2021, https://www.wbgu.de/fileadmin/user_upload/wbgu/ publikationen/hauptgutachten/hg2019/pdf/wbgu_hg2019_en.pdf.

odwaste (2019). *Foodwaste*, viewed 03 April 2021, https://foodwaste.ch/.

ngerling, C. (2018). "Action on Climate Change Mitigation in German and Chinese Cities—A Search for Emerging Patterns of Accountability." *Habitat International* 75: pp.147–153.

2. The City is a Videogame

Alina Nazmeeva

Mirror, mirror

In the epic adventure comedy *Free Guy*, to be released in 2021, the main character—rather ordinary bank teller—discovers that he is a non-playable character in an online computer game. When it comes to robberies or car crashes, he is a nonchalant bystander or a hapless victim, while other characters break into banks, race cars, or attempt to save the world through dazzling feats. At one point, the main character intervenes in a robbery and gets the glasses of a villain. At this critical transformative moment—undoubtedly a tribute to the science-fiction classic *They Live*—the main character puts on the glasses, and instantly sees an overlay of projected information on the space around him. The glasses augment his reality, with new items popping into his line of vision—across streets, along building facades, and all over the place. An interface with menus, buttons, maps, and inventories is displayed while background music plays in his ears. However, as he removes the glasses again, all of it stops. The music, the objects, the interface—all are components of the game experience, the game, being the reality of the world, in which he lives.

Free Guy is not only pertinent because it registers the relevance of online games to a mass audience. It also blurs the distinction between the experience of a virtual and that of a physical environment: as information and objects overlay the game space with the aid of his glasses. Fundamentally, if we remove a revelatory "this is a videogame" moment from the movie, it might as well be an augmented-reality adventure film set in Boston. In *Free Guy*, there is no conceptual "cyberspace", aesthetically or experientially distinguishable from the physical space—as is the Cartesian space of *Tron*, or *Hackers*, or the juxtaposition between reality and simulation in the *Matrix*. *Free Guy* instead, captures digital games, or virtual worlds as indistinguishable from tangible, physical reality.

ities, beyond their cinematographic portrayal, and particularly those heralded as being smart, profoundly blend with digital games. Increasingly, the same software is used for their urban design, management, and data analysis. Ubiquitous computing and Augmented Reality (AR) turn urban space into hyper-responsive game spaces. Online, digital games are getting realer than real—defined by hard-cash transactions, internal economies, and emergent social structures. Worldwide there are 2.5 billion gamers (Newzoo 2019), who attend concerts, meet friends, make money, buy and sell property, develop land, and have meaningful life experiences within online games.

Most of the concepts that fuel smart city rhetoric are envisioned and implemented in the form of digital games. Both cities (increasingly) and online games (by design) combine spatial systems with computer-mediated, and computation enabled, experiences. Where user-experiences of online games are defined by simulated three-dimensional environments, overlaid with information and interactive interfaces, the urban experience is increasingly mediated and enabled by software systems operating as non-diegetic parts of game interfaces.

The virtual worlds of online games are built around familiar, spatial-cultural archetypes: cities, streets, plazas, buildings, ecological landscapes, and infrastructures. These diegetic environments are overlaid with non-diegetic interfaces. In *Fortnite Battle Royale*, for instance, the non-diegetic interface includes the team's health bars, inventory of building materials, ammunition, building tools, a compass and mini-map accompanied by pop-up notifications and keyboard commands. This non-diegetic interface serves as a command-control interface connecting the player with the virtual world, so providing an awareness of their own, and their peers' status and location. This enables a player's actions through the provision of cues and elements of inter(action).

In online digital games, everything is part of a Graphic User Interface (GUI). With a GUI, images control what they represent. Operating as both tools and representations, the interface images become a specific genre of machine. (Bratton 2015). Images reveal the invisible and make it actionable. In the physical world, in a city, Google Maps presents an individual's location, and navigates their body through the city. Fitbit is, in its own way, a health bar, monitoring and displaying the physical health of the user. A smartphone—the meta-medium—makes reality malleable by virtue of providing an additional layer of information, displayed via GUIs of a multitude of apps akin to non-diegetic images overlaying a virtual world. Further, high-precision, geolocation-based AR applications, mirror the aesthetic and operational experience of virtual worlds; AR and VR, as used for construction, real-estate, entertainment and tourism, utilise the same design conventions and principles as digital games. Thus, by virtue of images, the experience and navigation of the virtual world and the experience and navigation of reality seem to have a striking resemblance.

Big Pictures

In the notoriously famous among urban planners digital game SimCity, the objective, as the title implies, is to design and manage a city simulation. The player—as a mayor—determines and monitors zoning, infrastructure and public services placement, tax rate, budgetary policy and other city-components. The player is assisted with a variety of interface elements that visualise the city's data, including population, transport, economy, real-estate data and even the mayor rating. Acting upon these data, the mayor finetunes and adjusts the city simulation. SimCity renders cities to be dynamic systems with feedback loops that determine their behaviour: after placement of the infrastructure and zoning areas, the buildings may or may not develop, the hike in of taxes may trigger citizens to leave. The simulation models and the feedback loops embedded in SimCity have been criticized as normative and quite North American centric, favouring suburban development and economic growth instead of green public spaces, density and social wellbeing. Yet the city-simulation, by the mechanics of playful interaction with the urban data renders SimCity a model for utopian urban management worldwide.

Smart city visions often connect urban systems with digital management tools into a seamless feedback loop. Cities across the globe use command-control interfaces for urban management. Rio de Janeiro's Operations Centre, designed by IBM, combines the data from over 30 city agencies, integrating real-time connection with city services and state departments. Over 80 screens are streaming real-time video from cameras placed at strategic points throughout the city, collecting satellite imagery, weather conditions, and other sensor data. The Operations Centre does preliminary simulations of large-scale events to anticipate any issues that might emerge (Gaffney and Robertson 2018).

However, looking at the city from above through the looking glass of reductive visualisation and simulation, it seems that those empowered to enact decisions operate as if, using videogame parlance—playing in a "god mode". In Rio, the distribution of surveillance cameras and sensors correlates to the spatial distribution of wealth; the data collected during large events are used to suppress protests; and citizens are virtually excluded from partaking in the decision-making process regarding data distribution, collection, and processing (Gaffney and Robertson 2018). By monitoring and managing them from the sidelines, this system renders underserved communities as NPCs (Non-Playable Characters or Non-Participating Citizens), like the character in Free Guy, or populations of SimCity.

he digital urban management systems akin to the Rio Operations Centre are increas-
gly produced with the software initially developed for, and used in, the videogame in-
ustry. In particular, real-time rendering game engines such as Unity (used in *Pokemon
o, Cities: Skylines, Hearthstone*), and *Unreal Engine* (used in *Fortnite, PlayerUnknown's
attlegrounds*), are used to design and operate digital twins and real-time urban data
odels. Digital twins of cities—which often take the shape of three-dimensional simu-
tions with an overlay of dynamic sensor data—are finding their application in global
ch capitals, from Singapore to New York (Liceras 2019; Keane 2019). A promotional vid-
o by *Siemens* (a competitor for Unreal Engine in the digital twin business) speaks of
igital twins as the technology which helps to "see, anticipate, experiment, plan, simu-
te and execute" product development of any kind (Siemens 2019). A digital replica is
eeded to improve the state of affairs in the physical space, make it more legible and to
elp to predict its future development.

he optimisation of rendering engines and improvement of ray tracing algorithms al-
w the production of complex photorealistic visualisations in real-time. The real-estate
ector, for example, uses virtual reality to test-drive and sell projects before they are
uilt (Athwal 2017). Other companies, merging digital representations with physical en-
ronments, use LCD screens to simulate windows (Olim Planet or Atmoth); or *A Cave
utomatic Virtual Environment* (known as CAVEs) and green rooms to showcase projects
imentel 2019; Aluminium 2017). A printed, still image of the future building no longer
ems enough when it is possible to have a stroll through the projected future—better
nd sharper than reality.

ode/Space 2.0 (Kitchin and Dodge, 2011)

an Doctoroff, a CEO of Sidewalk Labs, famously framed *smart city* aspirations as a
nought experiment: "What if we build cities from the internet up?" (Doctoroff 2016). He
nvisioned a city where the internet is a kind of foundation and brick-and-mortar space
f social and economic life. His vision for Quayside Toronto, and its larger innovation
an, not only implied the potential of ubiquitous connectivity, but referred to the so-
alled participatory and open nature of internet communication. Opposed to grand
eas and master-plan driven design, Doctoroff hinted at the collective creativity of Web
o migrating into physical space from-the-internet-up city: "We recognised that you
an never truly plan a city. Instead you can lay the foundations and let people create on
p of it" (Doctoroff 2016).

nline games are textbook examples of the Web 2.0 culture. In *Minecraft*—a digital
ayground constructed of clunky, cube-shaped blocks—players mine materials and
aft tools, objects, and environments. Each time a new game is started, a new *Mine-
aft* world is generated with terrain, biome, and village mobs (or populations of NPCs).
ayers can play on their own, with friends, or with strangers; collaborate and compete,
articipate in collective design projects or explore environments constructed by other

players. Players can also rent *Minecraft* servers, operating as de-facto system ad-ministrators. They are able to determine the rules, rights of use, and access privileges for different types of content on the rented server. Microsoft, the current *Minecraft* owner, does not impose any regulations on the servers. For kids, *Minecraft* has become a third-place; a social, creative, and educational platform outside of everyday routine and authority. It imposes different kinds of social demands where players not only have to collaborate on real projects but also perpetually negotiate social norms with respect to one another's virtual space (Thompson 2016).

In online digital games, legions of players spend thousands of hours developing characters and skillsets, building intricate spaces and solving problems, while the game developer and publishing corporations retain property rights over virtually all content produced by the players. In this instance, corporations operate as de-facto governor, owner, and creator of these worlds (Dyer-Witheford et al. 2006). Typically, access to the virtual world is only granted after players sign an end-user agreement prohibiting the use of any digital assets—which players have within the virtual world—beyond the scope of the game. The game developer, or publishing company, retains the rights to alter the game at any moment with no liability. They can change the number of items that might affect the virtual world's economy; redesign or remove objects and spaces at will. If the game servers go down and some items in a player's inventory disappear or get damaged, the developers are not required to return or restore them (Dibbell 2007; Castronova 2007).

Minecraft relies on player-driven creative production and social exchange. Similarly, in *Second Life*, every single item in the world is created by the residents themselves. The creative mode of *Fortnite* depends on its community of creators. The efforts of players create the cultural and social value of online games, yet, they have virtually no stake in what they make, while all profit generated by their labour goes exclusively to corporations.

No-Man's Land

Both online digital games and smart cities are software-enabled spaces populated by humans. In the case of the recently cancelled project Quayside Toronto and other of Google's smart city projects and urban design and management tools as built by Google-up, *Sidewalk Labs* holds exclusive power over all executive decisions, and controls the foundation of the smart city development—the software.

Online, everything is an asset. Online space is grounded in the concept of property ownership: from domain names and web-sites, to closed gardens of mobile applications, software licences, access privileges, to social media stickers, crypto-collectables, virtual clothes, pets, and virtual real estate in online games. In virtual worlds *erything is a part of the software, and software is a service—even if it looks and feels *e a thing.

*he rhetoric of Web 2.0 participation and crowdsourced remix culture is in conflict with *e reality that users themselves never own digital items. If one owns a Smart Home *vice, one doesn't own the software which makes it work. In fact, it is owned by the *mpany that made it, while users are granted a temporary right to use it (Dourish *16). The software is subject to change, at any moment, without the user's permission. *he Alexa Echo can become a social network hub, while at the same time, the iOS up-*tes from personal iPhones intentionally slow it down (Hill 2017; Greenfield 2017). In *e context of smart cities and online games, a lack in control over personal devices *ickly extends to a lack of control at a broader scale—that of social spaces, individual *uses, and entire cities.

*nline digital games operate as feedback mechanisms dependent on the data collec-*on of individual users. Game publishers and developer corporations can collect data *out every (inter)action of individual players. Furthermore, gaming devices capture a *ide array of biometric data; all online games track IP addresses and user's geolocation. * games such as *Pokemon Go* or *Minecraft Earth* fundamentally depend on high preci-*on geolocation tracking. Further, *Niantic* (*Pokemon Go* developer) tracks *Apple Health-* *API* to access the step count, energy use, or distance walked by users. In comparison, *culus* (producer of VR gear) collects the physical movement and dimensions of its users *ussel et al. 2018). Xbox Kinect captures facial features, body movement, and voice data *ussel et al. 2018). All of this information is used by default to make games work—for *stance, capturing the sequence of events for narrative progressions, or updating the *ser interface with new data in real-time (for example, your health bar, location, inven-*ry, etc). On top of that, user data are utilised to make targeted ads, personalised expe-*ences, and offer relevant digital content for sale.

*nart cities, too, are built on data. However, an appropriate solution for the governance * data which is satisfactory to all parties, in its protection of interests and privacy, has *t to be found. In recent years, a strong re-framing of urban projects, the city itself, and *e role of residents in its development has occurred. Data governance and privacy, lack * data transparency—on what, how, and by whom it is collected and used, are the most *ublicly debated issues with *Sidewalk Labs'* urban projects and tools (Korosec 2019). *hile *Sidewalk Labs* claim they have no plans to sell urban data to third-party compa-*es, their building of a location-based community enables the collection of valuable *anular data that can be used by the company.

*uilding the city from the Google-up with citizen data enables *Sidewalk Labs* to sell their *rban products—from mobile computing devices, network services, urban design soft-*are, to smart home devices—back to the community and city administration. Regard-

ing Quayside Toronto, the late reports by *Sidewalk Labs* claimed that only 25% of th
digital services for the project will be built in-house, it remains unclear under wha
conditions the remaining 75% would be purchased from third-party companie
Even if *Sidewalk Labs* laid out several promises concerning data privacy, it would no
oblige third-party companies to adhere to those same commitments (Sidewalk Lab
2019). Adequate institutions for the governance of urban data do not yet exist, whi
smart city experiments are continuing to drive discussions about their very desigr

The objective is fun

Smart cities are rarely portrayed as intentional territories of political participatio
and civic engagement. The role of the resident in the smart city is not that of a cit
zen. Instead, those residing in smart cities are occupants, users, consumers an
workers. By removing the inconvenience and hustle of urban routines from the u
ban experience, smart city, rather, becomes a place of entertainment, leisure, an
consumption (Dourish 2016; Greenfield 2014).

Both online digital games and smart cities are products of the experience econom
For both, fun is instrumentalised as a principal design objective. Moreover, akin t
the virtual worlds of online digital games, the private entertainment industry, suc
as theme parks and casino complexes, is at the forefront of using data collectio
and smart systems to enhance the visitor experience.

A prime example are the Disney World Resorts, capitalising on the smooth and le
surely fantasy experience of their visitors. In Disney World Resorts, restaurant host
know the names of visitors, Snow White knows their location, and snack carts con
veniently appear while pictures are taken and sent to personalised Disney account
With MagicBand, it is neither necessary to carry cash nor wait in line, food orde
come on time—leaving visitors only obliged to enjoy the park experience. Thi
seamless leisure experience is dependent on real-time data tracking via a system c
beacons distributed across the Resort territory and the MagicBands on the wrists c
the visitors (Kuang 2015).

From Potemkin-esque villages of new urbanist suburbia, desperately attempting t
imitate the visual language of Jane Jacobs' lively streets to tourist imploded histo
ic centres, cities too are becoming centres of consumer-driven leisure and enter
tainment. Hyper-programmed public spaces, crammed with ping-pong tables, wa
ter features, public art and gift shops, alongside pop-up markets and fairs, pervad
contemporary urban space. Overlaid with infrastructures of hard- and software
emerges the image of a fun and frictionless smart city.

Going back to digital games, all of them are predicated on the experience of bein
fun and engaging. They have to be aesthetically appealing, intuitively navigable

ave a strong narrative and be immersive. Online digital games immerse users in a
:ory, a social and economic system. All digital games have to have a strong sensory
nmersion via their informational, visual and auditory input. These worlds of im-
ges, signs and sounds obtain social and cultural meaning, and largely shape con-
:mporary culture. Before the explosion of social media and online gaming, the
:oncept of social space was linked to physical space. Business meetings were car-
ed out on golf courses; now they can take place in first-person shooters. Teenagers
·sed to hang out in their parents' garages; now they spend time in *Minecraft*.

igital games are predicated on spatial concepts: users get to explore the space,
1odify, occupy or even create it. Whether it is a single-player or multiplayer digital
.ame, for the user, the spatial exploration serves as a narrative device in which
•ace is an essential interactive component. The navigable space of online games
*Manovich 2001) blends visual culture, aesthetics, and computer science into a spa-
al system that operates with the tropes and affordances of both spatial and com-
uter-mediated interaction. The spatial and bodily simulations in virtual worlds are
ased on socio-behavioural conventions and interactions framed by physical space
:aylor 2002). You are on social media, yet you are in the virtual world.

he images of urban spaces, landscapes, and environments are similarly prone to
riving hyper-expectations of urban realities, just as celebrity culture is prone to
rive unrealistic standards of beauty. As cinema, photography, the advertising in-
ustry, and digital games increasingly utilise CGI technologies by distorting and
eautifying realities of the environments on display, their simulated worlds shape
1e cultural context of contemporary society. The image of urban or natural envi-
·onment is enhanced, edited, post-produced and digitally constructed.

igital games as well have a dialogic relationship with the urban space—as their
rtual cities are based on physical cities and their visions. Landscapes of San Fran-
·sco in *Watch Dogs II*, for example, distil the essence of the city by re-creating some
·f its prominent features, landmarks and spaces. Cities in *Grand Theft Auto* series
·e based on distilled versions of Miami, Los Angeles and New York; *Assassin Creed*
:ries are located in artistic recreations of Paris, London, Egypt and Libya. Tapping
·to the collective imaginary of those places alongside the particular historical pe-
·ods in which the games are set, virtual worlds in turn have a capacity to influence
1e cities and become rhetorical devices that update their collective image.

·he internet disappears
·t the 2015 World Economic Forum, Google ex-CEO Eric Schmidt is quoted as saying
·he internet will disappear. There will be so many IP addresses (...) devices, sensors
·nd things, that you won't even sense it. (...) It will be part of your presence all the
·me. A highly personalised, highly interactive (...) world emerges."

Cities are complex systems, in which social spaces economic markets, and everyday practices are increasingly governed and mediated by software. Smartphones, electronic cashier machines, car operating systems, airport and library scanners orchestrate the movement of humans and objects, creating codes and spaces of the everyday experience. Digital and internet-enabled technologies increasingly mediate and manage the large-scale infrastructures and spaces we live in: from smart cities to smart home systems (Kitchin and Perng 2016).

In virtual worlds, every item is intentional. The actions that can be performed with every item are pre-defined. If one wants to buy a t-shirt in a clothing store in *Second Life*, it can be tried on, purchased, put in a bag, or deselected—all displayed as options in a drop-down menu. Similar interfaces increasingly mediate and navigate everyday experiences worldwide. From banking chat-bots to self-checkout machines, to self-check-in hotels, the interaction between the individual and space is increasingly mediated by GUIs. In this sense, accidental interaction disappears as it is displaced by the declared function, mediated by specific yet arbitrary affordances of an interface.

The internet is everywhere

Both, the utopia of spatial computing and the great new world of the internet, at least in theory, bear the promise of liberation, efficiency, participation and creative expression for all. For both, the means to achieve these promises are the technological enhancement of social connectivity and environmental conditions. In John Barlow's 1996 "Declaration of the Independence of Cyberspace", the vision of the original, non-commercial internet was of a social space with the capacity to overcome social issues, in particular the seeming oppression by the regulatory authorities and governments of the businesses and individuals (Barlow 1996). The "new world" or "new frontier" are metaphors often used to describe the techno-utopian vision of the early internet, along with online digital games, Massively Multiplayer Online Role-Playing Games (MMORPGs), and virtual social worlds.

The virtual worlds of online digital games used to be perceived as uncharted territories, a terra nova, holding the promise and possibilities of building a new, better society from the ground up (Gunkel 2018). Although heralded as such in the mid 2000s, *Everquest*, *Second Life* and *World of Warcraft* never became alternative worlds with the ability to overcome the limitations of "meat-space". Contrarily, they became a part of ordinary life, merely replicating, exacerbating—or defining more precisely—the conditions of global capitalism. Presently, virtual worlds of *Fortnite* and *Minecraft* are described as platforms, social media, and third places (William 2019). By now, online digital games have become a legitimate sport, with massive stadiums built to host e-sports tournaments (Hughes 2019). Globally, digital goods are selling for hard cash. This is mirrored by the growth of a digital labour market

ithin the scope of online games, where users mine for gold and loot, primarily
sed out of China, Mexico, Romania, and Russia (Tai and Hu 2018).

early every new technology is perceived to possess the capacity for igniting pro-
und social change. Online games are no exception. Consider *Decentraland*—a
cently launched social virtual world, in which virtual reality and blockchain tech-
ologies are combined. In *Decentraland*, users claim to own and control virtual
nd, buy and sell parcels, buildings and goods. This fundamentally differs from the
pical online proprietary platforms, and online digital games, where the developer
publisher corporations own and control virtually all content (Decentraland 2018).

ch parcel of land in *Decentraland* is both a simulation of three-dimensional space
d a non-fungible token. Making it virtually impossible to copy the land, and the
sociated to it digital assets, makes the land and the goods finite commodities.
is intentional scarcity validates the economic value of virtual assets and puts the
dividual owner in control. A finite supply of land is arranged in a Cartesian grid of
e Genesis City, where each square-shaped parcel is adjacent to another parcel or
reets and public plazas (Waldorf 2018). Plazas and roads are akin to publicly
vned land (as they are owned and controlled by the Decentraland development
am), while private parcels and districts are owned both by individual users and
er collectives. Each user is free to design the space and has full control over their
nd. There is no censorship of the content embedded in the Decentraland gover-
nce structure. Conflicts between individual owners are left to social negotiation,
there are no other regulatory mechanisms to enforce decisions (Decentraland
18; Ordano et al. 2017)

e frontier rhetoric permeates *Decentraland*. Its neoliberal, techno-utopia rests on
e rhetoric of individual empowerment, land ownership, and the free-market. *De-
ntraland* portrays a new world, where individual spatial agency transcends top-
wn decision-making, while the design code and digital infrastructure (the grid,
nart contracts, graphic standards, etc.) are created and controlled by *Decentraland*
velopers. The individual parcels in *Decentraland* were built up by the owners
emselves and were not stitched into a continuous, immersive experience before
e public launch in February 2020. Today its landscape is defined by the property
es between the empty, half-built or finished parcels that have no relationship to
ch other.

similar rhetoric is widely utilised in the *smart city* imaginary. Masdar in the Unit-
Arab Emirates (UAE), Songdo in South Korea, Ordos City in China, and dozens of
her smart cities are built as centralised, private developments in "empty" and
nderutilised" areas (Greenfield 2014). These territories are de facto being removed
om government control as they are developed and financed by private multina-

tional corporations. They are often located within Special Economic Zones (SEZ), Free Enterprise Zones (FEZ) and other spaces of exception, where public policies are loos
blue-collar labour is exploited, and taxes are virtually non-existent.

Songdo, one of the largest privately developed cities on earth, was built on the blan
slate of reclaimed land from the Yellow Sea, within the Incheon Free Economic Zon
Originally planned for completion by 2015, it continues to be a work-in-progress. I
Songdo, developed areas and construction sites merge with wastelands. On an indivi
ual resident scale, everything can be managed and controlled remotely: from the ligh
and heating control in apartments, to opening doors and attending classes. Elevato
talk to garages; smart home systems talk to smartphones, cars mingle with traffic light
There are no rubbish collection vehicles—the pneumatic waste collection system spar
ning the city connects every apartment and building. Waste is recycled to generate ele
tricity which powers the city (Greenfield 2014, Poon 2018).

However, rather than being an actually functioning utopia, the city of Songdo instea
fulfils the role of a symbolic asset, to South Korea. The rhetoric defining Songdo is that
building a "new frontier" from scratch, while providing convenience and luxury for i
residents by implementing a responsive urban environment with command-contr
centres that manage the entire city, as well as individual residents. From the urba
planning and management perspective, Songdo offers efficiency and security throug
ubiquitous data collection and centralisation, while concealing unfavourable urban sy
tems such as those of waste management and water recycling. The image of a sustair
able, green, and sublimely high-tech future in Songdo is in stark juxtaposition to th
cultural imaginary of hustling, polluted, and overcrowded Seoul (Greenfield 2014).

Images used to market the vision of the smart city bear little to no resemblance to th
actual cities, or utopias-in-process defining today's existing smart cities. Rather, the de
scriptions, images, and manifestos, represent the vision of a utopia to come, in som
nebulous future. The city is described as a seamless experience of digitally enhance
environments, imitating the descriptions of those in online digital games. All objec
are talking to each other, all respond to you.

Yet, in fact, digital systems and devices are often comprised of piecemeal parts, designe
by rival corporations, incompatible with each other, buggy and erratic (Dourish 2016
The image of the seamless experience is merely a marketing strategy. Virtual worlds ar
by default orchestrated by code: they are buggy and lagging, the rendering engine
glitch, as most devices and software are incompatible with each other. Online games, a
nothing else, disrupt the fantasy of a real-time city.

The city as a videogame

Digital environments appear to provide a new, boundless frontier to explore and exploit. The internet and software dissolving into the physical environment turn the smart city territory into a whole new world infused and augmented by digital space. This new, digital enclosure of life posits profound questions. If all social space is digitally constructed and mediated, what is the difference between social space and cyberspace? How can the built-from-the-internet-up social space be truly participatory and egalitarian? How might the declarative and didactic interface imagind structures be subverted towards more accidental interaction practices?

Everything solid melts into (or finds its replica in) digital data—the very building block and native attribute of virtual worlds. Online digital games are growing more sophisticated and complex, visually appealing and immersive. Everyday practices that happen in the concrete, physical space of cities are increasingly mediated and governed by digital technology and communication. Digital games are becoming more massive, immersive, more social, and, with AR and VR more embodied and spatial. Practices once inherently spatial, and predominantly dependent on proximity and distance, migrate to the digital realm.

The rhetoric used to describe smart cities bears a striking resemblance to that of online digital games. From the perspective of a user or citizen, they both aim to deliver a convenient, accessible and delightful experience, while imposing granular control and orchestration by the administrator or state. From the scale of the system, in both digital games and smart cities, existing infrastructures of data collection and processing aim to operate as mechanisms of seamless feedback loops. The imaginary techno-utopia of the smart city—envisioned as a smooth, consumption-and leisure-driven virtual world, overlaid by digital systems, experiences, and a software-mediated space—coincides with the reality of large scale, capital-driven urban development, clear mandates, and closed-garden platforms. The two paradigms are folding together: the city becoming a videogame.

References

Athwal, N. (2017). "The Rise Of Virtual Reality In Real Estate." *Forbes*, viewed 07 February 2020, https://www.forbes.com/sites/forbesrealestatecouncil/2017/06/13 the-rise-of-virtual-reality-in-real-estate/.

Barlow, J. P. (1996). "A Declaration of the Independence of Cyberspace." *Electronic Frontier Foundation*, viewed 07 February 2020, https://www.eff.org/cyberspace independence.

Bratton, B. (2015). *The Stack: On Software and Sovereignty*. Cambridge, Massachusetts.

Castronova, E. (2007). *Synthetic Worlds: The Business and Culture of Online Games*. Chicago.

Dibbell, J. (2007). *Play Money: Or, How I Quit My Day Job and Made Millions Trading Virtual Loot*. New York.

Decentraland (2018) "Exploring Decentraland's LANDscape." *Decentraland*, viewed 07 February 2020, https://decentraland.org/blog/platform/decentralands-land scape/.

Doctoroff, D.L. (2016). "Reimagining Cities from the Internet Up." *Medium*, viewed 07 February 2020, https://medium.com/sidewalk-talk/reimagining-cities-from-the-internet-up-5923d6be63ba.

Dourish, P. (2016). "The internet of Urban Things." R. Kitchin and S.Y. Perng ed. *Code a the City*. London.

Dyer-Witheford, N., G. De Peuter, and I. Ebrary (2009). *Games of Empire: Global Capit ism and Video Games*. Minneapolis.

Gaffney, C., and C. Robertson (2018). "Smarter than Smart: Rio de Janeiro's Flawed Emergence as a Smart City." *Journal of Urban Technology* 25.3: pp. 47–64.

Greenfield, A. (2013). *Against the Smart City: A Pamphlet*. New York.

Greenfield, P. (2017). "Apple Apologises for Slowing down Older IPhones with Ageing Batteries." *The Guardian*, viewed 07 February 2020, https://www.theguardian.com/technology/2017/dec/29/apple-apologises-for-slowing-older-iphones-bat tery-performance.

Gunkel, D. J. (2018). *Gaming the System: Deconstructing Video Games, Games Studies, and Virtual Worlds*. Bloomington, Indiana.

Hill, K. (2017). "Surprise, Echo Owners, You're Now Part of Amazon's Random Social Network." *Gizmodo*, viewed 07 February 2020, gizmodo.com/surprise-echo-ow ers-youre-now-part-of-amazons-random-1796999365.

Hughes, C. J. (2019). "As E-Sports Grow, So Do Their Homes." The New York Times, viewed 07 February 2020, www.nytimes.com/2019/05/28/business/esports-are nas-developers.html.

Keane, P. (2019). "VR in CAD: Where Are We Now?" *Engineering.com*, viewed 07 February 2020, new.engineering.com/story/vr-in-cad-where-are-we-now.

Kuang, C. (2015). "Disney's $1 Billion Bet on a Magical Wristband." *Wired*, viewed 07 February 2020, https://www.wired.com/2015/03/disney-magicband/.

Kitchin, R. and M. Dodge (2011). *Code/Space: Software and Everyday Life*. Cambridge, Massachussetts.

Kitchin, R. and S. Y. Perng (2016). *Code and the City*. Routledge.

Korosec, K. (2019). *Sidewalk Labs' Blueprint for a 'Mini' Smart City Is a Massive Data Mine*, viewed 07 February 2020, techcrunch.com/2019/06/25/sidewalk-labs-blu print-for-a-mini-smart-city-is-a-massive-data-mine/.

Liceras, P. (2019). "Singapore Experiments with Its Digital Twin to Improve City Life." *Smart City Lab*, viewed 07 February 2020, www.smartcitylab.com/blog/digital-transformation/singapore-experiments-with-its-digital-twin-to-improve-city-life/.

anovich, L. (2001). *The Language of New Media*. Cambridge, Massachusetts.

dano, E., A. Meilich, Y. Jardi, and M. Araoz (2017). *Decentraland Whitepaper "A Block-chain-Based Virtual World."*

nentel, K. (2019). *Mixed-Reality Architectural Visualization Opens Doors for AEDAS Homes*, viewed 07 February 2020, https://www.unrealengine.com/en-US/blog/mixed-reality-architectural-visualization-aedas-homes-live.

on, L. (2018). "Songdo, South Korea's Smartest City, Is Lonely." *CityLab*, viewed 07 February 2020, www.citylab.com/life/2018/06/sleepy-in-songdo-koreas-smartest-city/561374/.

ssell, N.C., J.R. Reidenberg, and S. Moon (2018). "Privacy in Gaming." *SSRN Electronic Journal*.

ynaers Aluminium. (2017) *Avalon*. Viewed 07 February 2020, https://www.reynaers.com/en/avalon.

ewalk Labs. (2019). *Master Innovation & Development Plan Digital Innovation Appendix*.

ewalk Labs. (2019). *Toronto Tomorrow. The Urban Innovations. Volume 2.*

mens. (2019). "Why digital twins will be the backbone of industry in the future" [online video], viewed 07 February 2020, https://www.youtube.com/watch?v=Ob-GhB9CCHP8&ab_channel=Siemen.

, Z., and F. Hu (2018). "Play between Love and Labor: The Practice of Gold Farming in China," *New Media & Society* 20.7: pp. 2370–90.

ylor, T.L. (2002). "Living Digitally: Embodiment in Virtual Worlds." R. Schroeder ed. *The Social Life of Avatars*. London.

ompson, C. (2016). "The Minecraft Generation." *The New York Times*, viewed 07 February 2020, www.nytimes.com/2016/04/17/magazine/the-minecraft-generation.html?_r=1.

aldorf, T. (2018). "Designing Genesis City: Roads & Urban Planning." *Decentraland*, viewed 07 February 2020, https://decentraland.org/blog/platform/designing-genesis-city-roads-urban-planning/.

lliams, O. (2019). "Fortnite Isn't a Game, It's a Place." *Charged*, viewed 07 February 2020, char.gd/blog/2018/fortnite-is-the-new-hangout-spot.

3. Potentials of Open Weather Data in the Smart City Context:
An Exploration of Open Data from the German Weather Service (DWD) and Case Studies of Data-Driven Smart City Applications

Sebastian Meier/Inga Schlegel/Jochen Schiewe

Abstract

This paper assesses the open data infrastructure of the German
Weather Service (DWD). By discussing a series of exemplary projects that already use DWD data, dataset scenarios are explored
within the context of *smart city* developments. This is particularly
important as environmental changes brought about by climate
change pose new urban challenges. In the pursuit of resilient and
liveable cities, weather and climate data offer opportunities for understanding and adapting to unprecedented processes caused by
global climate change. This research hopes to spark a debate about
the potentials and challenges for working with DWD data resources, and inspire an active use of these datasets, thereby, promoting a
better understanding of climate and weather impacts on cities.

Introduction

Currently, the majority of the world's population live in urban areas (United Nations 2019). This proportion is projected to exceed
68% by 2050. Cities contribute profoundly to processes driving climate change (Moran et al. 2018; Creutzig et al. 2015) while their
inhabitants are left vulnerable to its consequences (IPCC 2014).
Cities are, for example, responsible for more than 70% of total
global CO_2 emissions (Johansson et al. 2012; IPCC 2014). At the
same time, climate change impacts from extreme weather, such
as droughts, heavy rains or flooding, pose risks for coastal cities,
threatening the livelihoods of densely populated areas. In order to
generate solutions to adapt cities to these extreme transformations, weather and climate data are essential for understanding
and predicting changing climatological phenomena. The emerging consequences of climate change in urban areas create an ur-
gency for finding adaptation processes to ensure more resilient
cities (GERICS 2015; adelphi et al. 2015). In most cases, data-driven
tools provide the necessary insights and understanding of climate
change and of its impact on urban areas. However, in order to
safeguard a transition towards greener and more resilient cities,
these tools need to go hand-in-hand with public policies and actions. The following sections discuss weather and climate data, as
the foundation of such applications, by examining case studies
using datasets to enable informed decision-making.

Weather Data

The data vaults of the German Weather Service (DWD) have been
open and publicly accessible for several years. In 2017, the German

1 https://opendata.dwd.de

2 https://cdc.dwd.de/portal

3 https://kunden.dwd.de/GPCC/Visualizer

4 https://maps.dwd.de

federal government revised the DWD legal mandate, updating i
portfolio, with the order to make the data accessible under a
open data licence (DWD 2017). Since then, the majority of data
the DWD portal are open, free, and publicly accessible. Only a fe
datasets require a charge, mostly those that apply to predictio
systems or domain-specific datasets like agricultural, aviation,
marine weather data. The open data is available under the feder
GeoNutzV licence (BMJV 2013), and accessible by requirement
correct attribution.

An FTP server1[1] provides access to DWD data by means of
browser, depicting a simple listing of folder contents. Descriptiv
meta-data provide additional information concerning, for exan
ple, spatio-temporal data resolution, or origin and processin
steps. Visualisations and tabular representations of specific dat
sets are also available through more accessible interfaces, such
the CDC[2] data and the GPCC data[3] (see Fig. 1). In addition, a subs
of datasets is also available from a GeoServer[4], providing individu
Web Map Services (WMS) and Web Feature Services (WFS) layers.

3.1 Overview of Available Data

This paper focuses on weather data in the context of smart ci
applications, primarily targeting historical (multivariate) sp
tio-temporal data, which have the greatest potential for practic
application. These datasets also represent the majority of dat
sets provided by the DWD. There are a few datasets, such as, for
casts in written language, which are omitted from the ensuir

Figure 1: Screenshot from the CDC
portal showing hourly station
observations of air temperature
2 metres above ground

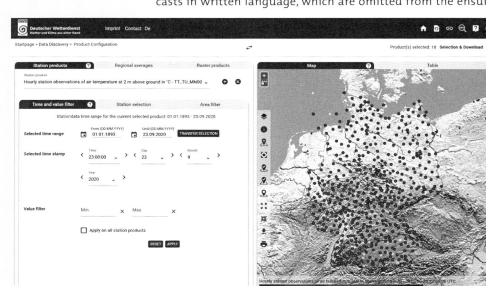

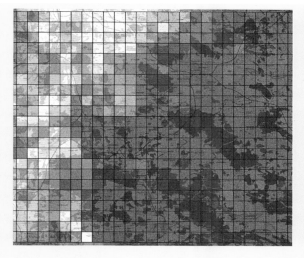

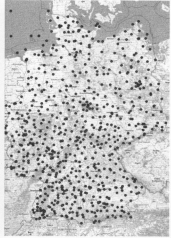

Figure 2: (Left): Exemplary 1x1km grid from the RADOLAN product.

Figure 3: (Right): Map of weather stations. Basemaps: © OpenStreetMap contributors

verview. The data are classified along the following lines: spatial-y, temporality, measurements or attributes, and formats—for hich a meta-data analysis of all available DWD datasets was unertaken. A list of the nearly 400 classified datasets can be found n GitHub[5].

1.1 Spatiality

rom a geographic perspective, the available data is categorised s follows:

1. Measurements from specific weather stations (see Fig. 3)
2. (Interpolated) national weather data in different spatial grids ee Fig. 2)
3. Aggregate-summary data for regions (e.g. federal states).

he dimensions of most grids are 1x1km cells; however, different roducts utilise a variety of grid types. Although the majority of ata applies to Germany, a few datasets have a European or global overage. The latter are mostly output from research collabora-ons with other organisations, such as GPCC products contribut-ıg to the World Climate Research Programme (WCRP) and the lobal Climate Observing System (GCOS) (Schneider 2018).

1.2 Temporality

he temporal coverage on station-related data varies as meteoro--gical measuring stations are continuously added, moved, and osed down. The earliest recordings date back to 1781, with a rise ı the density of data by the middle of the 20th century. Most of ıe available data, across all types, however, is from the past 30 ears. Temporal granularity varies strongly across different data-

5 https://github.com/sebastian-mei-er/dwd-opendata-analysis

sets, whereas high-resolution radio-sensor data is available at 30-second interval station-based climate data is published at 10-minute intervals; while most raster data range from hourly intervals to annual aggregations.

Particularly grid-data, yielding a high temporal density (e.g. hours), is available on the servers for a limited, historical period. Some historical datasets are only available for a certain time, usually because they are output from research or contract work funded by external sources, with an expiration date.

3.1.3 Measurements and Attributes
The types of attributes available with each product vary greatly, therefore the categories of: degree of processing and phenomena demonstrate the variety of available attributes. To attributes the degree of processing, raw sensor data and processed information are analysed. The raw information contains time series generated directly from sensors, which are rarely corrected for errors. The second group is categorised by processed data—in regard to cleaning and optimisation this primarily includes spatial and temporal aggregation and interpolation. Interpolation generates grid-data based on weather models, whereas aggregation provides summary statistics for temporal intervals. Within the category of phenomena, the most prominent attributes are: wind, radiation, temperature (air and/or soil), precipitation, sunshine hours, pressure, moisture (air and/or soil), clouds, vegetation, evaporation, solar radiation, and visibility. However, for the category of processed information there are noteworthy additional attributes, which represent calculated indices such as those for drought, thermal danger, days of bad weather heat, summer, frost, ice, etc.

3.1.4 Formats
The data of the DWD GeoServer, in addition to the FTP-service, is available in a variety of traditional spatial-data, raster (varies with product) and vector formats. Nevertheless, they constitute only a fraction of the overall datasets made available by the DWD. Data on the FTP-service itself is mostly the input for—or output of—meteorological software. The formats therefore often require additional software packages to ensure compatibility with GIS applications or other spatial-data tools Examples of such configurations include BUFR: Universal Binary Format for the Representation of Meteorological Data; RADOLAN: Radar-Online-Approximation; or GRIB: General Regularly-Distributed Information in Binary form. However, a few datasets cannot be read electronically, such as predictions in written language, or station lists in tabular formats.

3.2 Focus on Urbanity
In order to highlight these applications in the context of the smart city the relevance of the abovementioned datasets is briefly explained for urban scenarios.

2.1 Urban Climate Data

he DWD provides datasets specifically for urban contexts, for ex-
mple recent climate measurements for the station at Berlin Alex-
nderplatz and Freiburg central train station. Due to their location,
hese two stations do not adhere to World Meteorological Organi-
ation (WMO) standards, nonetheless, their recommendations
om the "Instruments and observing methods report No. 81" (DWD
018; Oke 2006) are considered. Whereas the majority of weather
ations are situated in urban peripheries, or open areas such as
irports, there are several urban stations that can be used for gath-
ring data, depending on the scenario. Within the city-limits of Ber-
n, for example, there are six stations with the capacity to collect
recipitation data. In the case of Hamburg, data is collected from
ree different stations. An overlay of geographical and land-use
ata, with locations of stations throughout Germany, showed that
any meteorological stations are located within cities and towns.

closer sampling of stations showed that particularly in small cit-
s, stations are often located on the outskirts. However, for cer-
in case studies, the data generated in these stations proves very
seful for monitoring or modelling urban weather phenomena.

2.2 Grid Data—RADOLAN

he weather stations document detailed information, often dat-
g back several centuries. The absence of available modelling ap-
roaches, however, poses a challenge for interpolating point data
or the expanse of an entire city. In this case, the grid-based
ata—often pre-processed and modelled by the DWD is a useful
lternative. The RADOLAN product stands for Online-Radar-Ap-
roximation. RADOLAN data provides 1km² grid-based approxima-
ons of hourly precipitation measurements in 0.1mm within Ger-
any (see Fig. 4).

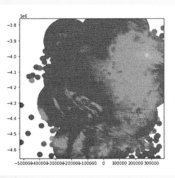 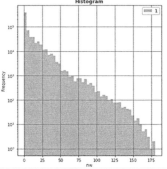

Figure 4: (left) RADOLAN data for 26 September 2020 13:50, brighter colours indicate more precipitation, dark blue indicates no precipitation.

Figure 5: (right): Histogram of the precipitation map on left (y: log scale), x-axis showing precipitation in 0.1mm.

This data is collected at 17 separate radar weather observatio stations across Germany. The aggregated data is then combine with more precise, spatially selective precipitation data from th other (non-radar) weather stations. The DWD model, usin point-data input of the latter stations, in combination with area measurements from the radar stations, creates an accurate ap proximation, with high spatial and temporal resolution. Due to it high spatial resolution, this dataset bodes especially well for ana lysing smaller spatial structures such as urban areas. The histor cal data goes back to 2005, and provides the opportunity for ir depth analyses of, for example, training models and generatin predictions. Compared to other data formats on the DWD ope data service, RADOLAN is relatively easy to utilise with GIS infra structures, since the data is available as ASC and BIN files[6].

6 An exemplary processing of DWD files is also available in the GitHub Repo.

The station and grid-data are only two examples of how th above-described sources can spur data-driven innovation in th smart city. The following section highlights five exemplary rea world case studies that integrate the resources of DWD ope data.

4. Case Studies

The previous sections provided an overview of the DWD open dat services. To further illustrate the potential and importance of suc datasets, the following section gives five examples of tools an services built around open weather data, concluding with an ou look for further usages, potentials, and challenges of open weath er data.

4.1 Urban Trees—Giess den Kiez

> Dataset: RADOLAN + Baumkataster Berlin
>
> Attribute: Precipitation
>
> Temporal Coverage: Last 30 days
>
> Target Audience: Citizens

Trees in cities have a positive impact on the liveability of urba spaces. In respect of the urban microclimate, they act as natura air conditioning systems (Rowntree 1986). At the same time, u ban trees are exposed to a variety of stressors, from an increas of sealed soil, to air and water pollution, in addition to genera impacts of climate change causing intensive heat periods wit low precipitation (Yang 2009; Dickhaut et al. 2019). In the hope c countering these drought effects, CityLAB Berlin[7] launched th

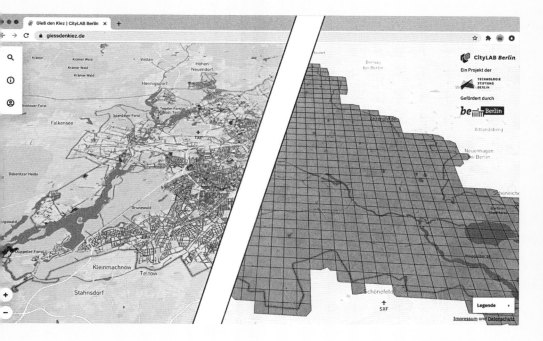

```
••• 🦒 Gieß den Kiez | CityLAB Berlin  ×    +
←  →  C   🔒 giessdenkiez.de
```

Figure 6: Screenshot of the web application Giess den Kiez (water your district), left: point visualisation of the more than 650,000 trees, right: visualisation of aggregate precipitation data (RADOLAN) for the past 30 days.

iess den Kiez (water your district) web application in the spring f 2020[8] (see Fig. 6).

he application is designed to focus on citizens. It visualises trees enUVK Berlin 2020) maintained by Berlin's public works depart- en. Citizens find additional metadata on each tree, with infor- ation on such factors as age; watering needs of particular spe- es; and the quantity of water individual trees already received om rainfall in the last thirty days. The underlying data derives om the DWD RADOLAN dataset. This precipitation data is col- cted daily and combined with statistics about publicly main- ined trees[9]. Additionally, the website displays data on watering atterns of local authorities, and the location of public water ells. Through interactive visualisations, citizens are encouraged water trees themselves. Upon registering on the website, citi- ns are able to contribute data on their watering activities which subsequently combined with the weather data. The overall ap- ication is open source and available on GitHub[10].

8 https://giessdenkiez.de

9 https://github.com/ technologiestiftung/ giessdenkiez-de-dwd-harvester

10 https://github.com/ technologiestiftung/giessdenkiez-de

4.2 Extreme Rain Events

Dataset: RADOLAN

Attribute: Precipitation

Temporal Coverage: Modelling from all historical data + Latest Data

Target Audience: Experts

11 The DWD's classification for extreme precipitation events (Starkregenereignis) is split into two models: 1) precipitation of 15 to 25 l/m² in 1 hour or 20 to 35 l/m² in 6 hours, refers to a weather warning scenario. 2) precipitation of > 25 l/m² in 1 hour or > 35 l/m² in 6 hours, refers to a bad weather scenario

12 see e.g., http://www.rimax-hochwasser.de/, https://www.fona.de/de/bekanntmachung-klimawandel-und-extremereignisse, https://www.climxtreme.net/index.php

Substantial research, which is in both the fields of climatology and meteorology, suggests that climate change will contribute to a a alteration in weather patterns (Madsen et al. 2014; Hawcroft et a 2018; Seneviratne et al. 2012; EEA 2019). Regional predictions fc Germany anticipate periods (KLIWA 2019) of prolonged drougt contrasting with a rise in extreme precipitation events[11]. Thes changes pose cross-regional challenges and are particularly prob lematic for urban areas (Castro et al. 2009) due to the density c building structures and the substantial ratio of sealed surface which create a range of problems associated with run-off (Pardov itz 2018). In recent years, the German federal government[12] ha funded a series of research programmes for analysing (Lorenz et a 2019; Einfalt et al. 2004), predicting, and forewarning (Einfalt et a 2009), uncertainty and resilience of extreme weather events in u ban areas (Kox 2018). Significant research, especially around topic of time-series analysis, modelling and prediction, is driven by pre cipitation products of the DWD, such as the radar data RADOLAN

4.3 Water Quality in Urban Rivers

Dataset: RADOLAN + Locations + Water Flows + Water Quality Measurements

Attribute: Precipitation

Temporal Coverage: Modelling from historical data + Latest Data for predictions

Target Audience: Citizens

The city state of Berlin offers public access to bathing locatior adjacent to rivers and lakes within the metropolitan area. Som of these locations, particularly along riverbanks, are prone rain-induced water pollution. The principal factor for such pollu ants is wastewater run-off from municipal sewer systems. Regu lar testing of bathing-water quality by the municipal administr. tion is costly and time consuming—from obtaining local sample to running lab analyses and making the results public can tak many days.

In order to provide citizens with a real-time insight into their wat quality, a research project led by the *Kompetenzzentrum Wasse*

Berlin[13] (KWB), developed a predictive model for deriving statistics on daily water quality for the most exposed bathing locations along the riverbanks (Seis et al. 2019; Seis et al. 2018). In its latest phase, the prediction system was scaled up to the federal level, to be accessed by states and cities throughout Germany[14]. The system calibrates on historical sample data and uses RADOLAN data from the DWD and from local water companies to generate predictions. In Berlin, generated predictions are publicly available to citizens in consultation with the *Landesamt für Gesundheit und Soziales*[15] (LaGeSo) via an accessible web interface[16] (see Fig. 7), developed by the *Technologiestiftung Berlin* (TSB).

13 Berlin Centre of Competence for Water

14 https://www.flussbaden.org

15 State's office for health and social affairs

16 https://www.badegewaesser-berlin.de/

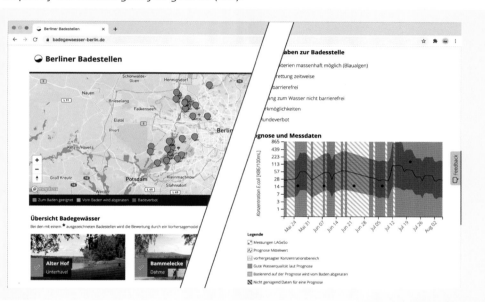

Figure 7: Screenshot of the web application *Badegewässer Berlin* (bathing waters Berlin), left: map and list view of all locations visualising current water quality measurements in a simple three-level warning system: good for bathing (green), bathing not suggested (orange), bathing forbidden (red), right; detailed view of a bathing location and a comparison of predictions and actual measurements.

.4 Urban Micro-Climate Modelling

Dataset: built Infrastructure data + models

Attribute: Wind, Temperature, Precipitation

Temporal Coverage: Latest data

Target Audience: Citizens

While the grid-data provided by the DWD bodes well for various analysis tasks, local higher-resolution models are required for the analysis of other objectives. Modelling weather and weather-related phenomena to include factors such as air pollution in urban areas requires more complex models and additional input data, such as built infrastructure (roads, buildings, etc.), elevation models, or vegetation. As a development extension of the PALM[17] system, the software PALM-4U[18] was initiated by a team at the University

17 https://palm.muk.uni-hannover.de/trac/wiki/palms

18 https://palm.muk.uni-han-nover.de/trac/wiki/palm4u

19 https://palm.muk.uni-hannover.de/trac/wiki/doc/app/iofiles/inifor

20 https://palm.muk.uni-hannover.de/mosaik

of Hanover, and allows researchers to simulate urban atmospheric boundary layers. The resulting simulation output is implemented for practical application in urban planning (Gross et al. 2020). In order to integrate real-world conditions for the simulation, weather data is imported into the system, for example, the development of an interface (INIFOR) for the DWD COSMO data[19]. The German COSMO-DE model is available as an open-data resource, in the format of a 2.8km grid, with various weather attributes, and historical time series dating back to 1995. Currently, the team behind PALM-4U is working on a graphic user-interface to broaden the accessibility of the underlying models[20].

4.5 Wind Energy Potentials

Dataset: COSMO REA-6 + SRTM + additional parameters
Attribute: Wind
Temporal Coverage: Modelling from historical data
Target Audience: Experts

Within the site analysis of planning wind turbines, multiple factors contribute to predictions about their efficiency. The complexity of the surrounding terrain influences energy yield estimates, in addition to other factors such as wind, ground, or building density. A rise in terrain complexity causes a decline in the accuracy of yield prognosis for planning wind turbines within an area. To facilitate the foundation of decision-making for stakeholders, while improving yield prognosis, the research project FAIR[21] provides a nationwide overview (Frank et al. 2020). Reanalysis data simulates the possibilities of future weather patterns, based on past events. The FAIR approach aligns wind-velocity simulation with the height of grid-based and regional COSMO REA-6 reanalysis data. Then the nearest data-values are transferred onto the geographic location of the planned turbine to estimate prevalent wind conditions (see Fig. 8).

21 https://www.fair-opendata.de/

Uncertainties concerning the data must account for a margin of error—in part from the simulation, and also from the terrain complexity and distance between the location of wind turbines and the closest COSMO grid point. Moreover, FAIR concentrates on two further scenarios demonstrating the value of meteorological data application: increasing safety and planning for open-air events by optimizing the response to weather hazards and estimating the occupancy rate of electric car-charging stations dependent on local weather conditions.

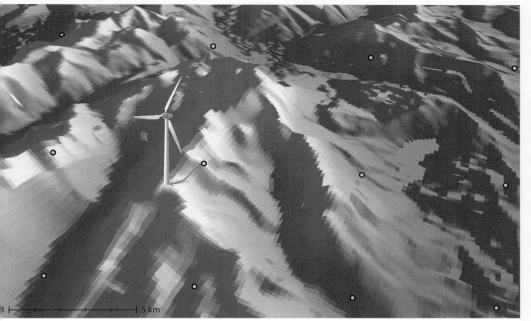

○ COSMO REA-6 gridpoint   ⟷ distance to closest gridpoint

Summary

n overview of the DWD open data infrastructure, highlighting ne wide variety of open data resources, formed the starting point f this research. By introducing a series of case studies, the poten- al of the examined datasets within the context of smart cities vas brought into focus. In conclusion, the opportunities and chal- ₁nges of classifying data, researching case studies, and working vith DWD data are identified (TSB: case studies 4.1 and 4.3; HCU: ase study 4.5).

Figure 8: Visualisation of estimated wind yield, from the distance between a wind turbine and its closest COSMO REA-6 grid point, including the surrounding terrain complexity.

₁ **Opportunities**

he case studies demonstrate that open weather and climate-da- ₁ hold significant potential in various applications of the *smart ity*—revealing two themes: modelling and visualisation. Most ₁se studies presented in this paper use the DWD data as input or model building. In particular, the availability of historical data llows for comprehensive, long-term model building. From these ₁odels, simulations and predictions are generated. Depending on ₁e model, the grid cells can remain at a low spatial resolution as ₁mployed by *Giess den Kiez*, or even scale down to building level ₁ata, as is in the case with Palm-4U. The models are combined ₁ith external data to generate new insights, ranging from air pol- ₁tion (Palm-4U) to water-quality for swimming (*Badegewässer*

Berlin). Less complex datasets like those from RADOLAN are also easily visualised (*Giess den Kiez*) to allow user interpretation of the data. Depending on the presentation of models, both themes can offer decision-making support to experts and amateurs alike in a variety of contexts—from urban planning to personal, everyday decision-making.

5.2 Challenges

Although the case studies highlight the importance of the DWD open data infrastructure, several barriers might prevent a broader public from accessing and working with the, albeit, open source data. Those barriers are mostly technical in nature, concerning the provision of open data. As described in the overview section, the data-formats, in addition to their spatio-temporal granularity, are exceptionally heterogeneous. This increases the difficulty for developers of working with the data, as every product requires distinct tools and processing steps. Besides, some datasets are huge in size, necessitating the download of several gigabytes. In other cases, data is in the format of written language, such as weather warnings, predictions, or station lists—and therefore non-machine readable. Some formats require in-depth domain knowledge and therefore make it difficult to gain insights into the data leaping across domain boundaries. Tools such as the GPCC visualiser hold potential for making data more accessible, and thereby leading users towards its application. However, an improvement in documentation and metadata would increase the usability of this treasure chest of meteorological data.

5.3 Concluding Remarks

This paper provides an overview of German weather and climate data, as supplied by the DWD under an open licence. Through real-world case studies, the potentials and importance of such datasets in the context of *smart cities* are highlighted. This research hopes to inspire and encourage further academic, corporate, and citizen data use to develop novel smart city applications in pursuit of liveable cities and urban resilience as the challenges of global climate change loom on the horizon.

he FAIR project is funded by the German Federal Ministry of ansport and Digital Infrastructure (BMVI; FKZ 19F2103D). The tyLAB Berlin is run by the Technologiestiftung Berlin and funded / the Senatskanzlei Berlin (Senate Chancellery Berlin).

eferences

elphi, PRC and EURAC (2015). "Vulnerabilität Deutschlands gegenüber dem Klimawandel." *Umweltbundesamt. Climate Change 24/2015.* Dessau-Roßlau.

MJV 2013). *Verordnung zur Festlegung der Nutzungsbestimmungen für die Bereitstellung von Geodaten des Bundes (GeoNutzV),* viewed 04 April 2021, http://www. gesetze-im-internet.de/geonutzv/GeoNutzV.pdf.

stro D., T. Einfalt, S. Frerichs, K. Friedeheim, F. Hatzfeld, A. Kubik, R. Mittelstädt, M. Müller, J. Seltmann and A. Wagner. (2009). "Vorhersage und Management von Sturzfluten in urbanen Gebieten (URBAS)" *Abschlussbericht,* viewed 04 April 2021, http://www.urbanesturzfluten.de/schlussbericht/schlussbericht/download.

eutzig, F., G. Baiocchi, R. Bierkandt, P. P. Pichler and K. C. Seto (2015). "Global typology of urban energy use and potentials for an urbanization mitigation wedge." *Proceedings of the national academy of sciences* 112.6: pp. 6283–6288.

ckhaut, W., G. Doobe, A. Eschenbach, M. Fellmer, J. Gerstner, A. Gröngröft, J. Kai, J. Lauer, C. Resisdorff, A. Sandner, S. Titel, A. Wagner and A. Winkelmann (2019). *Entwicklungskonzept Stadtbäume. Anpassungsstrategien an sich verändernde urbane und klimatische Rahmenbedingungen.* Dickhaut and Eschenbach ed. Hamburg.

WD (2017). "Geändertes Gesetz über den Deutschen Wetterdienst in Kraft getreten." *Pressemitteilung,* viewed 04 April 2021, https://www.dwd.de/DE/presse/ pressemitteilungen/DE/2017/20170725_dwd-gesetz.pdf.

WD, Climate Data Center (2018). *Aktuelle stündliche Lufttemperatur und Luftfeuchte, gemessen an Stadtklimastationen, für ausgewählte urbane Räume in Deutschland,* viewed 05 May 2021, https://opendata.dwd.de/climate_environment/CDC/ observations_germany/climate_urban/hourly/air_temperature/recent/BESCH-REIBUNG_obsgermany_climate_urban_hourly_tu_recent_de.pdf

A (2019). *Heavy Precipitation in Europe,* viewed 07. October 2020, https://www. eea.europa.eu/data-and-maps/indicators/precipitation-extremes-in-europe-3/ assessment-1.

nfalt, T., K. Arnbjerg-Nielsen, C. Golz, N. E. Jensen, M. Quirmbach, G. Vaes and B. Vieux (2004). "Towards a roadmap for use of radar rainfall data in urban drainage." Journal of *Hydrology* 299.3-4: pp. 186–202.

nfalt, T., F. Hatzfeld, A. Wagner, J. Seltmann, D. Castro and S. Frerichs (2009). "URBAS: forecasting and management of flash floods in urban areas." *Urban Water Journal* 6.5: pp. 369–374.

Frank, C. W., F. Kaspar, J. D. Keller, T. Adams, M. Felkers, B. Fischer, M. Handte, P.J. Marró
H. Paulsen, M. Neteler, J. Schiewe, M. Schuchert, C. Nickel, R. Wacker and R. Figura
(2020). "FAIR: a project to realize a user-friendly exchange of open weather data."
Advances in Science and Research 17: pp. 183–190.

GERICS (2015). "Cities and Climate Change." *Climate Focus Paper*, viewed 05 May 2021.
https://www.kfw-entwicklungsbank.de/PDF/Entwicklungsfinanzierung/
Themen-NEU/Focus-Paper-Cities-and-Climate-Change.pdf.

Gross, G., S. Raasch and B. Maronga (2020). "MOSAIK—Modellbasierte Stadtplanung
und Anwendung im Klimawandel", viewed 04 April 2021, http://www.uc2-
program.org/MOSAIK%20Verbundbericht%20[UC]2%20Phase%201.pdf.

Hawcroft, M., E. Walsh, K. Hodges and G. Zappa (2018). "Significantly increased
extreme precipitation expected in Europe and North America from extratropical
cyclones." *Environmental research letters* 13.12: 124006.

IPCC (2014). Climate Change 2014: Synthesis Report. *Core Writing Team*, R.K. Pachauri
and L.A. Meyer ed. Geneva.

Johansson, T. B., A. Patwardhan, N. N. Nakićenović, and L. Gomez-Echeverri ed. (2012).
Global energy assessment: toward a sustainable future. Cambridge.

KLIWA (2019). *Starkniederschläge—Entwicklungen in Vergangenheit und Zukunft.
Kurzbericht*, viewed July 2019, https://www.kliwa.de/_download/KLIWA-Kurz-
bericht_Starkregen.pdf.

Kox, T. (2018). "Unsicherheit in Warnungen vor hydro-meterologischen Extremereigni
sen." *Geographische Rundschau* 7.8: pp. 30–33.

Lorenz, J. M., R. Kronenberg, C. Bernhofer and D. Niyogi (2019). "Urban rainfall modifi-
cation: observational climatology over Berlin, Germany." *Journal of Geophysical
Research: Atmospheres* 124.2: pp. 731–746.

Madsen, H., D. Lawrence, M. Lang, M. Martinkova and T. Kjeldsen (2014). "Review of
trend analysis and climate change projections of extreme precipitation and
floods in Europe." *Journal of Hydrology*, 519.D: pp. 3634–3650.

Moran, D., K. Kanemoto, M. Jiborn, R. Wood, J. Többen and K.C. Seto (2018). "Carbon
footprints of 13 000 cities." *Environmental Research Letters*, 13.6: 064041.

Oke, T.R. (2006). "Initial guidance to obtain representative meteorological observations at urban sites." *WMO Instruments and observing methods report No. 81,
WMO TD* Nr. 1250.

Pardowitz, T. (2018). "A statistical model to estimate the local vulnerability to severe
weather." *Nat. Hazards Earth Syst. Sci.* 18: pp. 1617–1631.

Rowntree, R. A. (1986). "Ecology of the urban forest—introduction to part II." *Urban
Ecology* 9.3-4: pp. 229–243.

Schneider, U., P. Finger, A. Meyer-Christoffer, M. Ziese and A. Becker (2018). *Global Precipitation Analysis Products of the GPCC*, viewed 04 April 2021, https://opendata.
dwd.de/climate_environment/GPCC/PDF/GPCC_intro_products_v2018.pdf.

Seis, W., M. Zamzow, N. Caradot and P. Rouault (2018). "On the implementation of
reliable early warning systems at European bathing waters using multivariate
Bayesian regression modelling." *Water research* 143: pp.301–312.

Seis, W., S. Meier, M. Osaki, L. Hemmers, D. Sagebiel, S. Hoppe, A. Köhler, R. Gnirss, P.
Rouault and R. Szewzyk (2019). *Entwicklung eines Frühwarnsystems für die Berline
Unterhavel. KW Korrespondenz Wasserwirtschaft*, 9/2019 Berlin.

Seneviratne, S.I., N. Nicholls, D. Easterling, C.M. Goodess, S. Kanae, J. Kossin, Y. Luo, J.
Marengo, K. McInnes, M. Rahimi, M. Reichstein, A. Sorteberg, C. Vera, and X. Zhan
(2012). "Changes in climate extremes and their impacts on the natural physical
environment." C.B. Field, V. Barros, T.F. Stocker, D. Qin, D.J. Dokken, K.L. Ebi, M.D.
Mastrandrea, K.J. Mach, G.-K. Plattner, S.K. Allen, M. Tignor, and P.M. Midgley ed.
*Managing the Risks of Extreme Events and Disasters to Advance Climate Change
Adaptation.* Cambridge.

ange IPCC (n.d.). Cambridge, UK, and New York, NY, USA, pp. 109–230.

nUVK Berlin. (2020). *Straßen- und Parkbäume—Übersichten der Bestandsdaten*, viewed 07 October 2020, https://www.berlin.de/senuvk/umwelt/stadtgruen/ stadt-baeume/de/daten_fakten/uebersichten/index.shtml.

ited Nations, Department of Economic and Social Affairs, Population Division (2019). "World Urbanization Prospects: The 2018 Revision." (ST/ESA/SER.A/420). *United Nations*. New York.

ng, J. (2009). "Assessing the impact of climate change on urban tree species selection: a case study in Philadelphia." *Journal of Forestry* 107.7: pp. 364–372.

4. Taking Mixed Reality Serious: Co-Creation in the City of the Future

Hilke Marit Berger/Patrick Postert/
Imanuel Schipper/Anna E. M. Wolf

What if cities were to be created together? What if very different people, irrespective of their locations, were to develop ideas for cities jointly? What if everyone's knowledge mattered and contributed to changing the city? What if open-data and transparency were a matter of course? What if architects and planners worked together, with old and young citizens to draw plans for the design squares and districts? What if participation was taken seriously—as opposed to citizen involvement being synonymous with mere information events—what if it was in fact true co-creation? Imagine the city of the future could not only be envisioned and experienced, but also shaped collectively.

Participate

Fortunately, the car-friendly city's era—a planning perspective with the focus on the benefit of economised, maximum mobility—is over. Instead, today citizens' well-being is given top priority in urban planning. With that, urban digitalisation

rategies are also slowly moving their focus away from technical innovation alone
 developments oriented towards the needs of people and their participation in
ban society (BBSR 2017).

After all, participation is not merely a buzzword of recent decades, evoked across
ctions of society. It is a paradigm of our times. In other words, participation is an
evitable factor in any, and all future developments (Berger 2019). The striking suc-
ss of social networks is primarily due to the fact that people are given the means
 participate in a low-threshold and at a self-determined manner. However, the
assive societal divide, uncertainty, and the alarming political developments of
e present indicate that many people feel they somehow are not meant or are not
volved enough in political decision-making.

Opportunities for participation in urban development processes are especially
allenging, on various levels. In Germany, public involvement has been enshrined
 land-use planning law since 1971 (§3 BauGB). However, it consists only of formally
ganising discussions with citizens, while providing public feedback of plans. Ad-
:ionally, numerous informal participation procedures vary significantly in scope
d design. Often, people feel that they are not taken seriously in such processes
d that their ideas are unseen and unheard.

In many instances, it is about notifying the public rather than fostering active
rticipation and—above all—about giving people the feeling that they are taking
rt in a strategy, without actually questioning existing plans. The reproduction of
ese patterns parallels the problems of power relations in urban planning pro-
sses, which were already identified by Sherry Arnstein (1969) in her article *"Lad-
r of Citizen Participation"*.

llaborate

 this text is being written, the Covid-19 pandemic is producing effects that are
anging the entire world, showing—like a catalyst—the importance of digital
mmunication and how technical innovations already make working together vir-
ally possible. However, after six months of video conferencing, there is also an
 derstanding that real collaboration feels different from staring at a screen.

The idea of meeting in virtual worlds is not new and has been intensively re-
arched, for example, in collaborative virtual environments since the 1990s (Ben-
rd et al. 1995; Slater and Wilbur 1997). Driven by the new affordability of necessary
:hnical components, Virtual Reality (VR) is no longer just used by a few enthusi-
:s. In 2020, one could enter and move almost limitlessly within a virtual environ-
 ent (VE) with, for example, the use of a VR headset, interact with the environment
d each other, work together on whiteboards, talk to each other, present and
ange the content such as videos, graphics, or 3D-models.

Customised avatars represent individuals and are effortlessly created from a
 rson's photo, thus allowing recognition in real-life. Although the representa-
 n is often very abstract, and the transmission of non-verbal communication is

still limited to eye movements and gestures, hand movemen
have already become possible with a high degree of detail. Th
latter and the body movement allow us to interact naturally
the virtual world. Spatial audio helps visually impaired people
orient and physically impaired can move freely in the VE (Wo
2020).

Besides VR, Augmented Reality (AR) applications are also b
coming increasingly popular. Since AR only requires a smartphor
or tablet, collaborative spatial experiences are just a fingert
away. Citizens can easily use their own devices in participati
processes to visualise scenarios, comment on the spot with loc
tion-based discussion and opinion forming, as well as superim
pose the real and the digital world.

These are just a few examples that illustrate the possibiliti
of participation in social processes using virtual enviror
ments—allowing people to work together on their vision of th
future city, independent of time and place.

Co-Create

The joint research project PaKOMM rethinks participation ar
collaboration in planning and design processes. PaKOMM stanc
for participation, collaboration, and multimedia, and address
these issues by developing integrative solutions. By choosing
task-oriented approach, combining different visualisations th
have so far only been used in isolation and mixed media applic
tions, the project fosters a fact-finding experience of comple
spatio-temporal data. Following Donna J. Harraway's (201
"speculative fabulation" methodology and Jules Buchholtz's (201
"imaginary previews", PaKOMM proposes a techno-social scenar
that implements the breadth of existing media access to ser
various locations (on-site, off-site, and on-line) and different ter
poralities (synchronous, asynchronous) to generate diverse mod
of co-creation. Gamification elements enable an active and acce
sible involvement by citizens.

PaKOMM relies on experiences from participative plannir
projects at the *CityScienceLab Hamburg*[1], geo-data processing ar
visualisation at *g2lab*[2] as well as on Mixed and Virtual Reali
technologies at the *FTZ Digital Reality*[3]. In particular, the proje
Finding Places (2014) set a new standard in media collaboratic
involving interactive touch tables, displays, real-life database
and a moderated off-site workshop with citizens from the ci
(Hälker et al. 2018).

1 City Science Lab@HafenCityUniversity Hamburg https://www.hcu-hamburg.de/research/csl/

2 g2lab@HafenCityUniversity Hamburg https://www.geomatik-hamburg.de/g2lab/

3 Forschungs- und Transferzentrum Digital Reality @ HAW Hamburg https://www.haw-hamburg.de/ftz.digitalreality

4 For further information, see: https://www.hcu-hamburg.de/en/research/citysciencelab/research/cityscope/

chnically, PaKOMM provides easy access via smartphones and tablets in addition tools such as the CityScope and the *Location Finder*[4], combining them with VR adsets. The integration of annotations utilising proven and open standards of e Open Geospatial Consortium can retain available semantic information of the city models in PaKOMM's app ecosystem and ensure interoperability (Postert et 2021). This approach facilitates the swift extraction of relevant core statements Machine Learning and Natural Language Processing in the project.

e project enables co-creation in the following three settings:

a) Off-Site

oderated citizen workshops are combined with an interactive touch table and a nnected VR experience. Complex information (e.g., maps, infographics) on an in-ractive touch table is combined with 3D-printed models. The scenarios discussed e then implemented in real-time in an accessible VR environment. The workshop rticipants immediately enter the planned environment, and different versions n be debated at the data table, as well as modified or commented on in VR.

b) On-Site

rough an Augmented Reality (AR) application on their device, all interested par-s can view, redesign, and comment on the design proposals either alone, or in oups, directly on-site.

c) On-Line

ggestions and comments can be viewed and left on an on-line platform.

applications communicate and synchronise utilising a spatial-data infrastruc-re. The type of project visualisation and the complexity of the presentation are apted to the respective media (such as VR, AR, interactive touch table). PaKOMM expected to realise the first co-creation prototype design case study by the end of 22 for the planning of a green corridor in Hamburg's *Billbrook*.

e setting of the "off-site" workshop significantly differs from the usual sites at hich information evenings of traditional "participation processes" are held. In-ead, it is reminiscent of a contemporary theatre production, where the audience es not sit in a dark space, staring at the bright stage—but is invited to partake in e co-creation of the performance itself. The range of existing productions spans om the latter to city walks that involve phones, games, online meetings, or other nversation plays. All of them are creating settings in which the spectator (or user) comes a co-creator of the event they perceive—exactly as this is the case in the KOMM project. The citizen walking across the site with the AR tool attached to eir device reproduces a modern version of the 19th-century flâneur strolling rough the streets, re-constructing "his" city by his gaze (Schipper 2016). Both situ-ions express the co-creative, aesthetic, and highly political act of building and anging the town ourselves, with the help of some technological media.

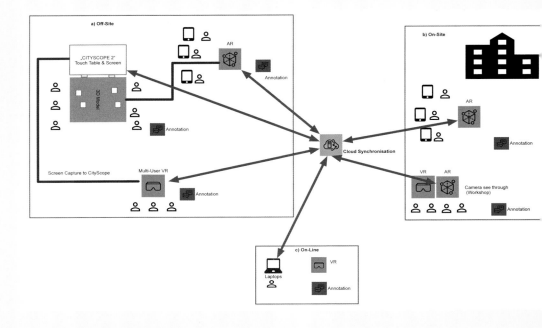

Figure 1: City of the Future

City of the Future

New media means new challenges and new possibilities alike. the city of the future, citizens will have the choice of whether the want to participate physically or virtually in the decision-makin process. Mixed Reality applications make it possible to experience complex data spatially and playfully, appealing to people wh may otherwise have little or no interest in participation proces es. Due to multimodality, the experiences are often perceived real and may have real-life impacts—which is both a challeng and an advantage at the same time. Concepts of participatio open governance, open data, and open source should apply digital technologies and new methods in an increasingly con plex world, without the overlooking the possible risks of manipi lation by the media used. Openness and transparency, as well awareness-raising for the consequences of data-driven urban d velopments, have to be key in every planning process. Alread large companies like Google with their *Sidewalk Labs*[5] are gettin involved in city planning processes. This will evolve in the futur VR headsets will play a crucial role in the collection of people data. In the city of the future, the division between our so-calle real and our digital world will be less and less important. By ta ing the possibilities of Mixed Reality seriously, citizens, as exper in everyday life, can work together with professional experts the processes of co-creating our city. Knowledge can be share

5 https://www.sidewalklabs.com/

cross borders as we learn from different points of view. To become resilient and adapt flexibly to new conditions, cities need novel ideas and unprecedented expertise. They need the expertise of many.

ferences

nstein, S. (1969). "A Ladder of Citizen Participation." *Journal of the American Planning Association* 35.04: pp. 216–224.

SR (2017). *Die Weisheit der Vielen*. Bürgerbeteiligung im digitalen Zeitalter. Bonn.

nford, S., J. Bowers, L.E. Fahlén, C. Greenhalgh and D. Snowdon (1995). "User embodiment in collaborative virtual environments." I.R. Katz ed. *Proceedings of the SIGCHI Conference on Human Factors in Computing Systems*. Denver.

rger, H.M. (2019). "Transforming Institutions or How to Shape the City Collectively." I.A. Finkenberger, E. Baumeister and C. Koch ed. *Amplifier and Complement*. Berlin.

chholtz, J. (2019). *Wem gehört die Zukunft? Wissen und Wahrheit im Szenario*. Berlin.

ker, N., K. Hovy, G. Ziemer (2018). "Das Projekt 'FindingPlaces'. Ein Bericht aus der Praxis zwischen Digitalisierung und Partizipation." T. Redlich, M. Moritz and J. Wulfsberg ed. *Interdisziplinäre Perspektiven zur Zukunft der Wertschöpfung*. Wiesbaden.

rraway, D.J. (2016). *Staying with the Trouble: Making Kin in the Chthulucene*. London.

stert, P., M. Berger, and R. Bill (2021). "Utilizing CityGML for AR-Labeling and Occlusion in Urban Spaces." A. Kamilaris, V. Wohlgemuth, K. Karatzas and I. Athanasiadis ed. Advances and New Trends in *Environmental Informatics: Digital Twins for Sustainability*. Nicosia.

hipper, I. (2016). "From flâneur to co-creator: The performative spectator." M. Leeker, I. Schipper, and T. Beyes ed. *Performing the digital. Performativity and performance studies in digital cultures*. Bielefeld.

ter, M., S. Wilbur (1997). "A Framework for Immersive Virtual Environments (FIVE): Speculations on the Role of Presence in Virtual Environments." Presence: *Teleoperators and Virtual Environments* 6.6: pp. 603–616.

olf, A.E.M. (2020). *Extended Reality für Collaboration und Meetings im Business-Kontext* (Master's thesis) Hamburg.

Workshop

Digest of the
City Science Summit
2010

. Mobility WITHOUT Noise: What is the Sound of the Future City? ow Does Mobility Planning Change if we Focus on Our Sense of Hearing rather han Our Sense of Sight?

Volfgang Gruel/André Landwehr

troduction

urrent discussions and representations of cities in the future are often deter-
ined by the visual senses. Depictions and pictures teeming with futuristic build-
gs, smart infrastructure, and new vehicles. However, humans have more senses.
How will the city of the future sound?" was explored as the central question of a
orkshop to which participants were invited. Exploring aspects of sound, and mak-
g use of computer modelling to illustrate potential outcomes, workshop partici-
ants created mobility models for the Grasbrook site, a new urban development
ea in Hamburg.

Workshop

The workshop goal was to explore new mobility-planning approaches with the focus on hearing, rather than visual perception. Briefly, a presentation of the topic was introduced. This included research results showing the impact of noise on quality of life by using soundscapes from the project "How does tomorrow sound" (Eisele et al. 2019), which enabled participants to experience the sounds of the city.

Participants were exposed to the sound of various environments in the city: a residential area, a busy neighbourhood, or an inner-city main road. Not only were sounds of the city transmitted as they are experienced today, but speculative scenarios for future soundscapes, such as a city of electric vehicles, were explored. Subsequently, a tool for visualising sound and audio was introduced after an awareness of soundscapes had been created.

Equipped with a new awareness of sound, along with tools for sound-mapping, the participants went on to design a city according to their acoustic desires. For this exercise, the site of Hamburg's *Grasbrook* was chosen. This development area, situated on a peninsula in the Elbe river, is of great significance for the future of the city's urban development. The site covers an area of 68 hectares, planned to accommodate 3,000 housing units for up to 6,000 inhabitants. The goal is to create a mixed-use, highly diverse, and dense urban district. It will create 16,000 jobs, providing space for commercial, office and residential uses, along with social infrastructure such as schools and sports facilities. The workshop participants were first asked to determine which (mobility-related) sounds they would like to hear on the Grasbrook and how, or if, the soundscapes should vary in different parts of the site.

Furthermore they developed ideas on how the proposals could be achieved: what kind of vehicles are allowed to go where? At what speeds? When, and how often are people allowed to drive?
In several phases, the participants created rules for each street on Grasbrook. The rules fed into a simulation program (Bocher et al 2019). Based on their inputs, the program generated maps illustrating the noise levels at distinct parts of the peninsula. Participants presented their strategies and results in order to discuss the different approaches.

he results demonstrated different strategies. For one group, mo-
rised traffic should, for the most part, be banned from the penin-
la in pursuit of achieving the optimal sound goals, while others
t rules for creating different sound zones on the Grasbrook. They
gulated the flows of traffic in different areas using access restric-
ons and dynamic speed limits. The zoning approach reflected the
acement of residential buildings and amenities.

Figure 1: Noise Design maps that
participants created and the
corresponding computed results

selection of corresponding design maps and computed results
ustrates the noise levels on the Grasbrook. The planning maps
ee Fig.1: first row) depict traffic planning: traffic density (num-
er of vehicles and speed) varies from low (green) to high (red).
he maps in the second row show the computed noise-maps:
ound levels increase from light green (45dB, comparable to aver-
ge home noise) to dark purple (>75dB, louder than vacuum
eaner or washing machine). These maps demonstrate the effect
 the different sound zoning approaches developed by the work-
hop participants. It became apparent to what extent the built
nvironment influences the urban soundscape.

Figure 2: Noise Design maps
presented by participants

Discussion

The multi-sensory approach received positive feedback fro[m]
workshop participants. It was clear that taking into consideratio[n]
aspects of audio perception is vital in planning for liveable citie[s]
Thus, participants expressed the need for considering multi-se[n]
sory aspects in city planning—particularly since planning exper[ts]
had expressed the view that sound plays a merely subordina[te]
role in planning processes. Those who took part in the worksho[p]
suggested a better integration of audio perceptions into intera[c]
tive city planning tools. They recognised that sound plays a cruci[al]
role in their general well-being. However, it was not clear wh[at]
makes a pleasant soundscape. Several participants observed tha[t]
not only is excessive noise harmful for the urban experience, b[ut]
that excessive silence also seems to negatively affect people's fee[l]
ings. This is to be explored further in detail.

Figure 3: Participants discuss which sounds they would like to hear on the Grasbrook

References

ocher E., G. Guillaume, J. Picaut, G. Petit, N. Fortin (2019). "NoiseModelling: An Open Source GIS Based Tool to Produce Environmental Noise Maps." *ISPRS International Journal of Geo-Information* 8.3: p. 130.

sele, J., J. Kieser, D. Rieger, W. Gruel (2019). "How Does Tomorrow Sound." *Hochschule der Medien*. Stuttgart.

2. Art WITHOUT Humans:
How do Digital Tools Influence Art in Urban Spaces?

Hosts: Sarah Adam/Hilke Berger/Vanessa Weber
Guests: Kathrin Wildner/Alsino Skowronnek

Figure 1 + 2: TAATM- Workshop

Data-intensive, machine-learning methods are omnipresent an increasingly adopted in everday life—from science, technolog and commerce to art, culture, and day-to-day urban living. Wit the rapid propagation of so-called artificial intelligence, countles questions emerge. What happens when the juxtaposition of dig tal and analogue dissolves? How does this process change our pe spective of the world? What defines creativity in a post-digital ag and how does the relationship between humans and machine influence artistic processes?

Who is acting?

"I am *The Amazing Augmented Tagger Machine* collecting you thoughts on art, artificial intelligence, public spaces, technolog and the power of non-human actors. Just tag me!"

The Amazing Augmented Tagger Machine (TAATM) explores th potential of artificial intelligence within the creative process c graffiti writing. It employs machine learning (ML) to generat ovel street tags that transcend traditional letterforms. Participants live-generate ieir own ML graffiti tags in the ghostly belly of a deep convolution neural net-ork, to then be transferred to an entire, real surface using paint. The result—an iteractive installation of ML augmented tags in physical space.

TAATM is a hybrid, custom-made piece of software and interactive installation ased on a deep convolution neural network, trained on a data set of ~1,000 anno-ited street tag images from across Germany. The model is able to generate new raffiti tags based on textual input from the audience. The final result is a contin-ally growing collage of tags, produced by participants in collaboration with the iachine.

iking TAATM by Alsino Skowronnek as a starting point for reflections about artifi-al intelligence, urban art, and public spaces, three seperate transmissions are ex-ored leading to the question: are we indeed witnessing art without humans?

st Transmission: From the streets to Instagram
What is the relation between tagging and taking pictures of tags?
How does this process transform aspects of individuality?
To which aesthetic modifications does this transmission lead?

cond Transmission: From Instagram to *The Amazing Augmented Tagger Machine*
How does Instagram, as a medium, influence the process of collecting data?
What is the decision-making role of the programmer or artist if there
is no raw data?
How does the analogy of human and machine learning appear?

iird Transmission: From *The Amazing Augmented Tagger Machine* to the wall
In which relation does the human factor (experience, skills etc.) emerge?
How is the wall as an artefact something other than a decorative backdrop?
What happens in the transmission from the street, to an artificial wall,
to tagging as a form of communication?

3. Cities WITHOUT Privacy: How Ecosystem Awareness Can Improve the Design of Interconnected Smart City Services

Christian Kurtz/Florian Wittner/Mattis Jacobs

Digital services are increasingly interconnected and the vision of digital cities embraces these connections in pursuit of delivering a powerful and seamless experience for citizens. However, the complexity of networks explodes, and data quickly diffuses into a vast network. This workshop provided three perspectives of information systems, law, and ethics in combination with the research project "Information Governance Technologies" initiated in Hamburg. The research question of how, and in which context smart cities should make use of (personal) data was addressed in detail. Also, the advantages and trade-offs of privacy protection by use of personal data were discussed alongside presentations of practical solutions.

With about twenty participants, including external guests, students, and academics, case studies in diverse contexts were discussed. This included a range of topics such as e-scooters and waitlist apps, smart museums, cyclist barometer and trackers. The potentials of strengthening ecosystem-awareness to enable esponsible development own of smart city services were illustrated. The diversity in data recipients and data uses in digital cosystems were highlighted, while raising awareness and suggesting approaches for mitigating the risks of data diffusion in mart cities. Emphasis was placed on discussing problems resulting from cities, as public actors, cooperating with private ompanies, who provide the hard- and software for smart city pplications while pursuing their financial interests.

the discussions, two major findings surfaced. First, many participants who did not have a background in informatics were unware that substantial amounts of personal data, especially location data, are processed for various purposes. Also, participants ave (temporary) acceptance to the secondary use of their personal data, beyond the scope of the provided service, to support ty planning, for example. However, the use of personal data for urposes such as advertising should be restricted. Overall, the orkshop fostered intensive and fruitful interdisciplinary discussions, contributing to a holistic view of the complex issue of smart ty ecosystems.

4. Session Series on Informality:
1. Development WITHOUT Formality
2. In/Formality WITHOUT Bias
3. Hamburg WITHOUT Borders

Lisa Reudenbach/Marie Malchow/
Luis Alberto Alonso Pastor/Markus Elkatsha

Populations around the world are urbanising at an unprecedented rate and scale. 2050, 68% of the world's population will live in urban areas, adding another 2.5 billio people to the current global population and with nearly 90% of this increase takin place in Asia and Africa (UN DESA 2018). These urban centres are facing the monu mental challenge of providing adequate infrastructure and essential services to burgeoning population seeking jobs and services in cities. By 2050, it is predicted tha 3.5 out of the 9.1 billion global residents will live in informal or unplanned commun ties (UN-Habitat 2016). However, informality is not limited to housing but is also a aspect of labour or service provision, such as transportation, education, and healt care. In sub-Saharan Africa, for example, the informal economy accounts for 55% c

DP and 80% of its labour force (African Development Bank 2013). In many of these instances, traditional infrastructure solutions are too costly, inefficient and slow to implement, and may cause the displacement of large numbers of people. In situations where governments are not able, or willing to provide essential services for urban residents, many communities rely on informal processes for the provision of basic needs. Their solutions and negotiations range from informal to formalised practices, co-existing with and underpinning formal practices and institutions.

In this session series, four grassroots initiatives from around the world explored innovative (informal) solutions to challenges such as waste management, urban planning, health, safety and security, along with other fundamental needs.

Enhancing Liveability Through Resource Efficiency – Lessons from Cairo

The research of Heba Khalil from Egypt employs urban metabolism as a lens through which to investigate resource efficiency, as an essential criterion to achieving the UN Sustainable Development Goals (SDGs). Comparing two diverse districts in Cairo, one formal and the other informal, the research examines current resource flows, from source to sink, regarding materials and mobility. Through the fieldwork, the research debunks common misconceptions regarding informal areas and systems, questioning the need for scaling up successful practices of informal systems. Furthermore, it proposes several systemic strategies that can improve resource efficiency on the level of the individual, the building, the district, and the city.

Human City Project

Michael Uwemedimo presents the Human City Project in Port Harcourt, Nigeria, where formalised urban planning strategies consist merely of ignoring or bulldozing. The Human City Project combines media advocacy, urban planning, and litigation to help residents of informal settlements imagine, plan, and build their neighbourhoods in new and sustainable ways. With the means to tell their stories by film, on-air, in court, and by charting local realities on maps and describing their visions urban action plans, these communities are changing lives and shaping their city.

Creating Opportunities for Crime Prevention

Mayra Gamboa presented good practice examples of safety and security in informal settlements in Mexico. The case study area, Lomas del Centinela is a community of 5,400 inhabitants located between two contrasting neighbourhoods: one very poor and one wealthier. Here, the University of Guadalajara together with a local NGO employed initiatives such as art workshops, urban agriculture, and community dining to support children and their parents to develop work skills, moving them away from practices of everyday violence. It also includes an urban literacy programme promoting the acquisition of values, attitudes, and behaviours that contribute to establishing a culture of respect within the community.

Figure 1: Project workshops
© Luis Alberto Alonso Pastor

4. Urban Solutions at the Intersection of Formality and Informality

In his research, Jyotimitra Raghuvansh from India notices that distinctions between the formal and the informal are not sharp, but fuzzy, complex and multi-layered. The solutions to rogue urban problems are, in fact, often found in this space—where informality meets formality—and where innovation happens across sectors, scales, and stakeholders. In India, one can learn from many such examples in healthcare, waste management, or access to potable water at the community and grassroots level with urban solutions emerging at the intersection of people, providers, and policymakers.

In this session series, a diverse group of researchers and practitioners from Germany and around the world discussed the lessons learned from these case studies, the advantages and challenges of informal solutions, and the possibility of supporting, developing, or replicating such successful cases. The group debated the feasibility of formalising informal processes, and the extent to which that is desirable. The group also reflected on the conceptual validity of distinguishing between the formal and the informal, concluding that focus should instead be directed at functionality. Formality was perceived as something cultural and often imposed, while informality is frequently linked to questions of legality and legitimacy. Changing this common perception was seen as a means of societal redistribution of power and resources.

In the final part of the session series, the group went outdoors to experience informality in Hamburg. In a walk through a neighbourhood led by a local non-profit called grenzgänger e.V. (Grenzgänger 2020), the group explored a different side of Hamburg, one that is invisible to a majority of the city's residents:

Figures 2 + 3: Project workshops
© Margaret Church

They look after children, they clean, and they build hous-—there are numerous people in Hamburg who are involved everyday life, but who actually should not be here according the law: undocumented migrants. No matter whether they e looking for accommodation, starting school, on their way to ork, or in case of illness—coping with everyday life, in this sit-ation, requires good organisation. The guided walk informed out the life situations of people without papers, debunking yths and stereotypes. It offered the opportunity to get to ow networks and organisations by—and for, undocumented igrants. The tour is based on the organisation's research, sup-emented by experiences from NGO work, police interviews d the work of other researchers" (Grenzgänger 2020).

ferences

ited Nations Department of Economic and Social Affairs, Population Division (2018). *World Urbanization Prospects: The 2018 Revision*. New York.

ited Nations Human Settlements Programme (2016). *World Cities Report 2016: Urbanization and Development—Emerging Futures*. Nairobi.

ican Development Bank (2013). *Recognizing Africa's Informal Sector*, viewed 9 Janu-ary 2020, https://blogs.afdb.org/afdb-championing-inclusive-growth-across-africa/post/recognizing-africas-informal-sector-11645.

nzgänger | forschung & training (2020). *Menschen ohne Papiere in Hamburg*, viewed 8 January 2020, http://www.grenzgaenger-hamburg.de/stadtrund-gaenge-hamburg/menschen-ohne-papiere.

5. Data Chain WITHOUT Chained Data: Rethinking Bottom-up Data Collection in Utilising Digital Process Chains for the Built Environment

Organisers
HCU Hamburg BIMlab:
Daniel **Mondino**/Emiliya **Popova**/David **Ehrenreich**
MIT Media Lab:
Suleiman **Alhadidi**/Christian **Jara Figueroa**

The workshop addressed the role and value of data in shaping and maintaining the built environment from a bottom-up approach that is, data gathered by people in their homes and at work. Two scenarios investigated the processes for creating and maintaining building-level datasets of existing and new buildings: a city, with workflows of data gathering systems; and places without such systems. These datasets have the capacity to be managed by 3-D Building Information Models (BIM). Additionally, the workshop explored the multi-level application and relationship of the gathered datasets: from plot to city, and within the context of a data ecosystem.

amework

igital data, sometimes called big data, is an emerging field of innovative techno-
gy offering novel ways to extract value from the tsunami of newly emerging inforation. By 2020, estimates predict that there will be more than 16 zettabytes
6 Trillion GB) of useful data (Turner et. al. 2014).

Opportunities for data collection and data management concerning processes
 urban planning and construction are rapidly evolving. Today, a variety of sensors
 n collect information about the built environment and the people occupying it,
 cluding factors and characteristics such as solar activity, sun shading, air quality,
 ind speed, humidity, air temperature, and quality of drinking water. All these fac-
 rs influence well-being and perception both in- and outdoors. Besides, informa-
 on about the use of various digital devices allows us to analyse and predict hu-
 an behaviour and well-being in different environments.

These developments pose new challenges for the manner in which data is
 ared and integrated into digital process chains of the built environment.

The question of the future of defining and managing data for the public good
 d private interest was also raised.

ethodology

 e workshop participants were divided into three groups of between eight and
 ne members and received a brief lecture explaining the conceptual framework.
 rticipants were presented with sensing technologies with which various societal
 allenges, related to issues of the environment, transportation, housing, safety
 d healthcare, are addressed (see fig. 1). Each group was free to decide on their
 wn challenge, based on the outcome of a tailored discussion session. They sug-
 ested datasets for addressing the selected challenges by explaining the dataset
 arameters that would affect the quality and/or performance of the built environ-
 ent.

Societal Challenges (examples)

 ased on the diagram below (fig. 2), participants were presented with the following
 e challenges:

1. Find a societal challenge.
2. What kind of data can be used to tackle the challenge?
3. Which dataset is privately owned and which is open source?
4. How can the datasets be of personal value on an individual level?
5. How can the data create value for the public (plot, neighbourhood, and city-scale)?

Challenge Examples

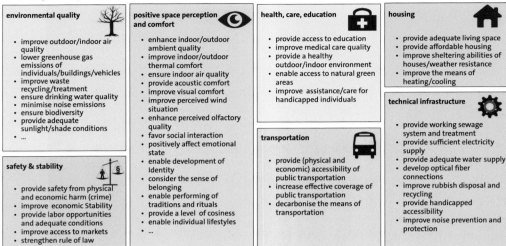

Figure 1: Societal Challenges (examples)

Figure 2: Digital Data Process Chain in Built Environment

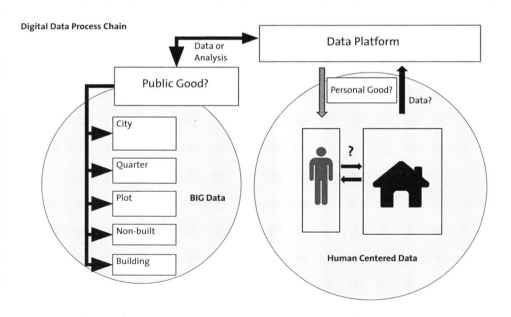

Outcome

During the 60-minute time slot, the three parallel group discussions diverged in various directions. Most groups engaged in a discussion about the benefits of data, distinguishing between private and public benefits. In one group, it quickly became clear that companies were already collecting most of the necessary data for the purpose of private interest, while the importance of trust and transparency in data management was the focus of another group. The third group discussed issues related to the reliability of data and potentials of its real-time use.

Three messages emerged as an outcome of the workshop:

No Data Platform Without Trust

What data is shared? Where is it shared?
Who has control over it?
The premise of sharing data is fundamentally based on trust. Without trust, it is impossible to establish a common ground for collaboration. Trust is related to issues of control and security. Where there is a lack of trust, data sharing suffers from the tragedy of the commons, as people reap the benefits of a data chain without sharing their private data. In this sense, digital data sharing platforms must become a tool for generating trust in order to build a public good. However, the most challenging question remains that of who runs and controls this system. The workshop participants identified three potential agents for controlling the system: private companies, governments, and non-profit organisations. Regardless of the controlling agency, there is a need for public policy regulation of the data ecosystem, as it affects data transferability across platforms.

No Shared Data without Shared Values

In which ecosystem is data shared? For what purpose?
Where can it be shared?
Shared values are essential for the process of decision-making. All individuals, however, act according to their own value system based on personal understandings which are firmly (inter)connected with understandings and beliefs collectively shared as a society. This principle also remains valid within the emerging data-driven digital reality. Data ecosystems for the built environment, for example, can exist for the public good only if based on shared values. Therefore, the question how these shared values are identified and shaped should be seen as a critical discussion to be continued. Blockchain technologies, for example, were identified already during the workshop as a potential answer to this challenging question.

No Objectivity Without Subjectivity

Is one conscious of their wants and needs? How reliable is personal perception?

How can subjective data be made objective?

New digital tools hold the potential for making subjective data objective by quantifying it to a point from where reliable and tangible measurements can be extracte
However, how reliable are subjective data? Subjective perceptions are not static bu
subject to variation according to mood and changing circumstances. Is it possible a
ways to be conscious of our needs? Can objectivity exist without the reference(s) c
subjective perceptions?

References

Cavanillas J.M., E. Curry, W. Wahlster (2016). "The Big Data Value Opportunity."
J.M Cavanillas, E. Curry, W. Wahlster ed. *New Horizons for a Data-Driven Economy.*
Cham.

6. Arrival WITHOUT Departure

Jan Barski/Benedikt Seitzer

All participants in the "Arrival WITHOUT Departure" workshop had moved to a different country at least once in their lives. In total, twelve people who met this criterion joined the workshop. They were divided into two separate groups in order to ensure that every participant was interviewed for long enough to gather the desired information. The goal of the workshop was to identify and discuss the advantages and disadvantages of arriving in a new city, and to understand which factors influence the ease or difficulty of leaving a place.

Each participant received a "game sheet", on which they answered questions relating to moving to a foreign country. In general, they were asked to provide information on the positive and negative sides of their moving adventure, giving their responses in the form of anonymous statements. The participants were asked to provide several aspects of information about the move: their age when it occurred, the purpose and reason for the journey, as well as any special circumstances or feelings associated with it.

Next, the answer sheets were randomly distributed, leaving each person in possession of the response sheet of another, to them unknown, participant.

This opened the second phase of the workshop in which participants played a guessing game based on the sheets they were holding. They first read the statements out loud and then responded with a commentary—either from their own experience of the mentioned city, or based on their assumptions about the place. Then they had to guess to whom among the other players the sheet which they held belonged. After the author identified themselves, they were joined by the moderator, and the player who had made the guess, in a brief interview, discussing the mover's experience and process of arriving and departing.

In the subsequent, third phase of the workshop, the interview results were categorised into positive and negative areas by the participants. The figures below illustrate these findings. Statements as to what makes arriving in a place more difficult are evenly distributed within four areas. Unsurprisingly these consisted of: bureaucracy, understood as the tedious administrative and legal processes necessary for gaining permission to live and function in a place; a chaotic housing market; language barriers; and discrimination. Worthy of note is the fact that the aspect of discrimination not only applied to those participants who identified as people of colour (POC) moving to countries with a primarily Caucasian population, but also affected a white European moving to Asia, where they experienced positive discrimination, based on the difference of their skin colour. Infrequent, however, were mentions of the cost of housing, unreliable public transportation, and pollution.

The most significant factor which contributed to an easier arrival was the category of "international agreements". The workshop participants overwhelmingly decided that nothing facilitate moving across a border like a set of well-intentioned agreement between two countries. This sentiment was most easily identifiable in interviews with persons who had experienced moving within the European Union, however not exclusively. Other mentions of positive factors included university affiliations (those who moved to study found their arrival noticeably softened), English-language fluency (theirs, and that of the local population reliable public transportation (enabling mobility), an enticing cultural offer and an international character of the arrival city.

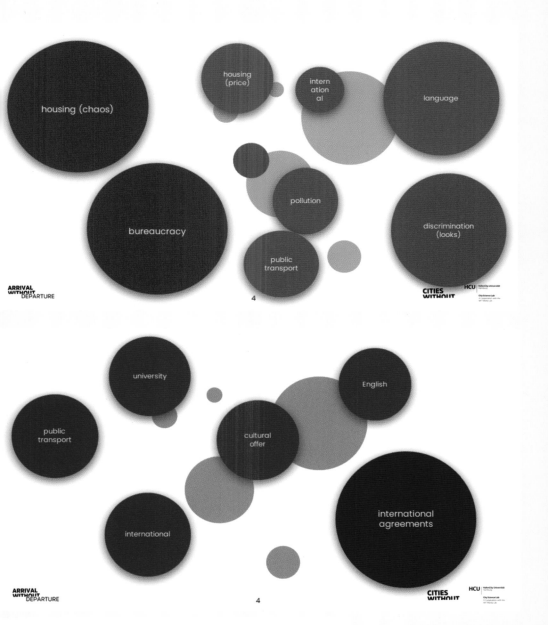

Figures 1 + 2: Outcomes of the workshop game.

7. Smart WITHOUT Culture? How Cultur Impacts Smart Cities

Contributed by Jens Bley and Martin Niggemann
Host: Jens Bley
Co-Hosts: Marianne Ping Huang/Lorna Hughes/ Gianluca Fabbri
Experts: Henning Vöpel/Rainer-Maria-Weiss/ Uwe Jens Neumann/Kay Hartkopf/ Anais Wiedenhöfer

Challenge

Indices for smart cities across the globe lack a recognition of the role of culture. Generally speaking, culture is commonly sub-sumed in indicators of education or citizen well-being, hence being a soft contributor. This challenge investigated impact perspectives—social, economic, innovation—and their measurability based on experiences from European cities. As exemplified by Rome, the culture-centric and tourist-flooded eternal city; Glasgow, the first European Capital of Culture in 1990; Aarhus, Europe's Capital of Culture in 2017; and Hamburg as a living laboratory and urban testbed.

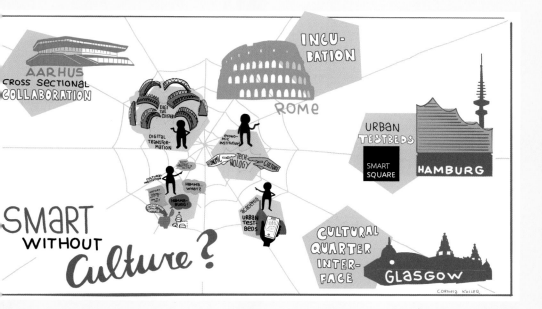

Figure 1: Smart WITHOUT Culture?

Graphics: Cornelia Koller

ormat

n a rapid-impact-assessment workshop opened by state-
ents from city officials and experts, the perspectives of po-
ential impacts such as cross-sectional collaboration, incuba-
on, urban testbeds and cultural quarter interfaces, were
resented and discussed. Additionally, views on strategic im-
acts, contributing activities, stakeholder relationships, and
easurability of impact where exchanged.

Figure 2: Perspectives of potential impacts

iscourse

n essence, five significant realms of impact were identified:
igital Cultural Democracy, Cultural Urban Narratives, Cross-
ectional Collaboration, Cultural Quarter Interfaces and the
elationship of Culture, Technology and Economy.

ECONOMIC IMPACT	SOCIAL IMPACT	INNOVATION IMPACT

Location Attractiveness / Quality of Life / Culture and Technology Interaction / Networks & Digital Hubs / Perception of Cities as pre-condition	Quadruple Helix / Citizen Engagement / Cultural Maker Spaces / Open Cultural Data / Local Knowledge / Transparency & Learning of Cultural Production	Start-ups & Incubation / Attract Creative Talents & Economy / Open Innovation Cross Sectional Collaborati Local Actors

Figure 3: New Role of Cultural Institutions as Facilitators for Smart/ Wise Cities

Economic impacts include location attractiveness, networks an digital hubs, culture and technology interaction, and the (self-)pe ceptions of cities as a pre-condition.

Social impacts include quadruple helix citizens and civic soc ety engagement, cultural maker spaces, open cultural data, loc knowledge, transparency and the learning of cultural production Innovation impacts include start-ups and incubation, the attrac tion of creative talent, open innovation, cross-sectional collabora tion and local actions.

In this sense, cultural institutions can and should assume th role as (co-)facilitators for the co-creation of impact in smart citie